FLIES NOW THE SPIRIT

FLIES NOW THE SPIRIT
Alone Yet Complicit

Light Verse

Keith and Elizabeth Stanley-Mallett

ARTHUR H. STOCKWELL LTD
Torrs Park   Ilfracombe   Devon
Established 1898
www.ahstockwell.co.uk

© Keith & Elizabeth Stanley-Mallett, 2013
First published in Great Britain, 2013
All rights reserved.
No part of this publication may be reproduced
or transmitted in any form or by any means,
electronic or mechanical, including photocopy,
recording, or any information storage and
retrieval system, without permission
in writing from the copyright holder.

British Library Cataloguing-in-Publication Data.
A catalogue record for this book is available
from the British Library.

ISBN 978-0-7223-4310-4 Cloth-bound edition.
ISBN 978-0-7223-4311-1 Paperback edition.
Printed in Great Britain by
Arthur H. Stockwell Ltd
Torrs Park   Ilfracombe
Devon

Previously published poems by the same author:
Little Traveller – Pumpkin Publications
Conspiracy of Faculties – Poetry Now, Forward Press, 1994
Yielding Forms – Poetry Now, 1994
One, That are We – Poetry Now, 1994
Two Minutes of Silence – Anchor Books, 1994
A Norfolk Winter Sunset – Poets England Series, Brentham Press, 1994
Come Silently to Me – Poetry Now, 1995
To the Eye – Poetry Now, 1995
World Wide Conceded Nationally – Poetry Now, 1996
Three Times Twenty – Poetry Now, 1996
I Believe in Betjeman – Poetry Now, 1996
Emotive Machine – Poetry Now, 1996
Essence of Time – Poetry Now, 1996
Poetic Visions – Poetry Now, 1996
Once Upon a Time – Poetry Now, 1996
The Red Fox – Anchor Books, 1997
Soul Winds – Poetry Now, 1997
Across a Timeless Threshold – Anchor Books, 1999
Mrs Batholomew's Door – Anchor Books, 1999
Electronic Life – United Press, 1999
Under An Indigo Moon – Arthur H. Stockwell Ltd, 2009
Beneath Rose-Lemon Skies – Arthur H. Stockwell Ltd, 2009
Before the Rainbow Fades – Arthur H. Stockwell Ltd, 2010
Between Night and Dancing Light – Arthur H. Stockwell Ltd, 2010
Beyond the Last Horizon – Arthur H. Stockwell Ltd, 2010
Upon a Past and Future Path – Arthur H. Stockwell Ltd, 2011
Odd Wit and Other Bits – Arthur H. Stockwell Ltd, 2011
Gilded Images – Arthur H. Stockwell Ltd, 2012

FOREWORD

BOOK IX

Although we did not envisage writing further books of verse, my wife, Elizabeth, and I found our pens hovering over blank sheets of paper again. We found there was still so much left to see, feel and express feelings about, be sides, we did not like to see our desks and pens idle.

So would like to offer you our last work entitled *Flies Now The Spirit*. We hope you will enjoy it.

Keith Stanley-Mallett

I have poured out so much emotion in this book, it portrays my feelings and I hope they are conveyed to the reader. This book is vastly different from any of my other works covering many more subjects.

Elizabeth Stanley-Mallett

All poems are original and previously unpublished.

INTRODUCTION

This book completes a series of ten volumes of verse written by both myself and my wife Elizabeth and this will be the last and final work from us both.

We hope that over future years our work will be of some interest to those of you of a poetic and philosophic disposition.

We would like to thank all those involved with the production and publication of our work over the years.

Keith Stanley-Mallett

I hope my contribution to this book will be a little different from those previous as it will be the final book of verse we shall write. In this volume I have tried to convey my very own feminine ideals and morals without preaching. I believe I have achieved a quantity of poetic work that is in my own opinion more in keeping with modern thinking. Some are narrative in nature, which I trust will promote more interest to readers generally. Any poem is only as good as its subject and writer.

Elizabeth Stanley-Mallett

Part I

Light Verse

By

Keith Stanley-Mallett

CONTENTS

Fingers of Light	15
Summer Solstice	16
English Evening	17
One or 'Tother	18
England In Midsummer	19
Dawn Star	20
The Waiting	21
Tiny Worlds	22
Igniting the Darkness	23
Smoke	24
Humanities Song	25
Dandy Seeds	26
Upon a Silver Aspen	27
As the Weather Will	28
All That Is Seen	29
Coat of Many Hues	30
What Others See	31
The Listless Spirit	32
So Radiant	33
Weather-worn	34
Decorating the Fences	35
The Weather We Share	36
Travelling Spirit	37
A Spark on the Wind	38
So, To Their Retreat	39
Mischief Was His Name	40
Mask of Life	41
Flies Now the Spirit	42
Flies High the Flag	43
Quicker By Far	44
Veil of Secrecy	45
The Haunting Winds	46
Truth	47
Where the Spirit Has Trod	48
The Wildest Field-Green	49
All at Once	50

Sky and Garden Green	51
Secrets Lost	52
The Receiving Mind	53
We, Tree, Field and Flower	54
A Constant State of Flux	55
A Million Gods?	56
Their Spirit Travels On	57
The Last Dance	58
Washing the Dust Away	59
Cottage, Meadow and Hedges of May	60
Cloudscape	61
Like Sun, Like Song	62
Beauty of the Land	63
As August Becomes September	64
A Delicate Balance	65
Expectation	66
On Silent Wings	67
Life's Thorns	68
Neither One	69
Upon Summer Warmth	70
Transient Spirit	71
Good Intentions	72
Alone In a Field	73
Air, House and Fen	74
In Secrecy	75
Imagination	76
To Mellow Close	77
Day After Day	78
Old Laws and New	79
Fruit, Leaf and Bloom	80
As a Gift	81
Just a Few	82
To Reason	83
Fingers of Life	84
Golden Days	85
Chimneys of the Shire	86
This Colourful Land	87
Spider Town	88

Bramble, Elder and Apple	89
Somewhere, Sometime	90
As If Upon an Ark	91
The Reason Why	92
Humanity	93
The Breath	94
Nature's Daughters	95
Both High and Low	96
September's Face	97
The Indulgent Spirit	98
Season to Season	99
The Roads of England	100
Half a Laugh and Half a Tear	101
When Clouds	102
A World of Thought	103
A World of Light	104
Upon Two Legs	105
Bedroom Bears	106
On This Earth	107
Meadow Home	108
Compliance	109
In Secrecy	110
When We Were Young	111
Secret Dreams	112
A Servant of Time	113
Born In Nature's Lair	114
Verdant Green	115
Elkie, a Friend	116
Borne on Time's Wings	117
In Full Worth	118
Companions	119
Of Thought	120
October 31st	121
As a Seed	122
The True Dawn	123
The Father of Them All	124
So Precarious	125
Topaz and Diamond	126

Celebrated Season	127
To Seek	128
Pickle	129
Destructive Rain	130
Bright Light	131
Damp Days	132
This Fair Day	133
Mists of the Mind	134
Silent and Unseen	135
Morning Sunlight	136
White Upon White	137
Song of Life	138
There	139
For But a Moment	140
So Much So Little	141
All or Nothing	142
The Pages	143
The Air of Life	144

Fingers of Light

Darkness slowly fades away
    With dawn's approaching fingers of light,
'Til the golden orb's full splendour
    Bursts forth, full star-bright.

Thus in answer to the dawn
    Twilight shadows at dusk deepen.
And darkening clouds are set aglow
    By moonlit fingers, seeking.

Summer Solstice

The longest day
    Is here to stay
But, for a few hours longer,
    With sun or rain
Summer's refrain,
    Her warmth a little stronger.
Moonlit, the night
    Soft as a sigh
Brushed with silken breezes,
    Caresses the mind
And heart to find,
    Each summer solstice pleases.

English Evening

When I look across the land
And see nature's exquisite hand,
    Of upland, dale and meadow
The woodland and cottage mellow.
In the light of evening sun
    When the summer day is done,
There is nowhere on this earth
    To compare, beauty, of this worth.

One or 'Tother

When the shadow falls at last
Shutting off the light of being,
Will I, to anger and rage
Or peacefulness be feeling.
Will I know that I am dead
No longer to feel or know,
Or in spirit fly to where
    The temporal mind can grow.

So, 'tis one or the other,
To be dead as a doornail
No longer thinking, seeing,
Touching, inhale or exhale.
Or swift as a beam of light
Be transported to far realms,
Where enlightenment ensues
    And in learned truth, dwell.

England In Midsummer

England in midsummer
    Is so contrary,
For the changing mistress
    Of her weather be –

Likened to a child
    In temperament,
Who, so diverse her way
    Fair and inclement.

Thus betwixt sun and rain
    Breeze or thunderstorm,
England in midsummer
    To us, just the norm.

Dawn Star

The morning star, gem bright
    Hangs 'twixt dawn and night,
Amidst the fading shadows
    And fine gold of the light.

A sister of the earth,
    Mysterious of birth,
Messenger in the east
    In beauty and in worth.

Companion to the moon's
    Pale crescent, that soon
Will, as part of day
    Be lost at height of noon.

Thus, both in secret lay
    Beyond the sun's fierce ray,
'Til eve's falling shadows
    Spell night and end of day.

The Waiting

The waiting to start school,
The waiting to be a teenager,
    The waiting.
The waiting to start earning,
The waiting for your wages,
    The waiting.
The waiting to get married,
The waiting for your wife,
    The waiting.
The waiting for a family,
The waiting, good times and strife,
    The waiting.
The waiting for midlife crisis,
The waiting for retirement,
    The waiting.
The waiting for your pension,
The waiting and confinement,
    The waiting.
The waiting now you are old,
The waiting when you are ill,
    The waiting.
The waiting every day,
The waiting, long hours to fill,
    The waiting.

Tiny Worlds

Within each drop of rain
    A singular world of H_2O
What microscopic denizens
    Are swimming to and fro?

Taken from the oceans deep,
    Drawn up to the stratosphere,
Cast by wind and cloudy realms
    Each small watery tear.

Gathering like a waterfall
    Together and yet each alone,
To rain upon the land beneath
    Tiny worlds of H_2O.

Igniting the Darkness

Brightly glows the new-dawn sun
    Lifting the shadows of clinging night,
    Pouring warmth over all below
    Igniting the darkness in light.

Thus, warming the human heart,
    Awakening the slumbering mind,
    Full challenging the spirit
    Once more to seek, to learn, to find.

The life-giving solar warmth
    Beaming from this, our radiant star,
    Is the very same matter
    That created, who we are.

Smoke

The chimney pots
Along the tops,
    In groups of four
    Above each door.

Decorate ridge
Roof, tile and ledge,
    And send their smoke
    Above the folk.

To mingle on high
With winter's sky,
    As row on row
    The fumes did flow.

To drift and add
Noxious gas,
    With cold grey fog
    Creating smog.

As years ago
Each chimney flow,
    The air, made ill
    As all smoke will.

Humanities Song

What is this single spark?
    This individual spark of life?
A thinking entity
    Unknowingly born in pain to cry.

Created by those who
    Arrived before, indulging the mind
And body in passion,
    Thus to bring forth, one of their kind.

One small living flame thrust
    Into this turbulent world of strife,
Just one of billions
    Forever forthcoming, day and night.

Another spirit brought
    To join earth's ever growing throng,
Perchance gifted, thereby
    Lifting humanities future song.

    Be it a Jane or John.

Dandy Seeds

Dandy seeds of Lyon
　　Full fine of head,
Waiting for the breeze
　　Its seeds to shed.

Sending each seed to find
　　That point of earth,
To once more bring to life
　　A dandy plant's birth.

To colour the wayside
　　A golden hue,
When each Dandy-Lyon
　　Brightly grew.

Upon a Silver Aspen

Silvered leaves of aspen
Like crystal flakes, reflect
    The light in gentle waves
    Of movement, nature perfect.

A thousand leafy facets
Catching the seeing eye,
    As this living art-form
    Brightly shines beneath the sky.

A living hoard of treasure,
Shining silver'd pieces
    Upon a silver aspen,
    Beauty, that so pleases.

As the Weather Will

Clouds like sugar puffs
    Lay high in the sky,
Edged by smoke-grey
    Dark billows that lie –

Upon the horizon,
    Casting deepening
Shadows over all,
    Beneath the sweeping –

Expanse of the sphere
    Heralding the rain,
As the weather will,
    Command the change.

Nature decides when,
    The weather for us
Warmth, sun, cold or wet,
    Will do as it must.

All That Is Seen

I look across the meadows
    Rich grasses and wild flowers,
Bounded by the dense thicket
    Of hawthorn, may, rose, endow'd.

And lift my eyes above, where
    Thatched rooftops can still be seen,
Of cottages neatly set
    Edging the old village green.

Beyond, the woodland rises
    A thrusting band of shadow,
Sanctuary for many
    A fox, rabbit or black crow.

The land beyond is rolling
    And all that is seen are fields,
That dip'n rise, furrow'd or green
    'Til country to town yields.

Coat of Many Hues

Once I met a lady
I thought could be my wife,
    With happiness and love
    All the days of my life.

Sadly, this could not be
She'd a-coat of many hues,
    Changing her demeanour
    With lashing tongue too.

No matter what I did
To soothe her cares away,
    She so spat and did fume
    And her venom did flay.

I knew we had to part,
So I upp'd one day
    By early light of dawn,
    And took myself away.

What Others See

When I look each day to see
    The many views around me,
The world in all its glory
    As told in every story –

Do I see what others see?
    Nature in all its beauty,
The sky, the sea, the mountains,
    The cities, squares and fountains.

Or does each of us unknown,
    Unaware and thus alone?
See a world quite different
    From others, yet be content?

Will we ever know the truth?
    Do others see what we do?
Is it exactly the same
    The colour, the sun, the rain?

Perhaps then, variations
    In shade, hue, colouration,
But we, each of us, our sight
    Holds true, whatever is right.

The Listless Spirit

Softly hissed the fan
As it turned back and forth,
Pushing the humid air
    With electro-motive force.

Stirring the atmosphere
Around this darkened room,
Ruffling old thin curtains
    Hanging in the fly-sought gloom.

Bottles upon the table
Empty of the beer contain'd,
With cigarette ends
    And a pizza slice, unclaimed.

'Til dawn evokes once more
Another day of heat,
Mind sapping and listless
    The spirit, can face defeat.

So Radiant

The eastern star
    Full secret, rises,
In early hours
    From the horizon.

A lonely star
    Yet diamond bright,
So radiant
    A face, in the night.

And still she gleams
    In the light of dawn,
Rising higher
    'Ere the sun is born.

Down long ages
    A traveller's guide,
Evening star
    Does by daylight, hide.

Weather-worn

Weather-worn, the fence tops
    That stand the boundary round,
    Enclosing the garden
    Where tranquillity is found.

Weather-worn, the seating
    Once placed beside the path,
    A place to sit and rest
    View the beauty of each plant.

Weather-worn, the old bridge
    Spanning the ornate lake,
    Once was the centrepiece
    That times, now past, did state.

Weather-worn, the old house
    Which once was grand and alive,
    The shutters now broken
    Only ghosts for tea at five.

Decorating the Fences

Yellow, pink and cream,
    Upon the probing tendrils
Of honeysuckle,
    Seeking to further fulfil –

Nature's urgency,
    So spreading its scented life,
Across the timber fencing
    Reaching, in warm summer light.

Perfuming the air,
    Such a joy to the senses,
A noble beauty
    Decorating the fences.

The Weather We Share

Although 'tis summer
    There's a chill in the air,
Temperatures dropp'd
    And the sun is not there.

The weather we share
    Is a motley affair,
With sunshine and rain
    Depressions, then it's fair.

Such troublesome days
    At all times of year,
With winters so mild
    As if spring, would appear.

The heat in July
    And in August the same,
Can be stifling
    'Tis the sun then, we blame.

Even the weather
    A topic much used,
Yet always surpris'd
    And ever in the news.

Travelling Spirit

The mind in concord
With the travelling spirit,
    Reacting as one
    Both equally complicit.

Whether temporal
Or inborn, spiritual,
    Both mind and feeling
    Become inspirational –

Where 'ere the spirit
Does seek and thereby to fly,
    To realms far distant
    Or in beauty confide –

The secrets of nature
And of far places unknown,
The travelling spirit
    Discerns the essence as shown.

A Spark on the Wind

The spirit of life
    Is such a small flame,
    Like a spark on the wind
    Blown hither like rain.

Full harried by life
    Each glowing small spark,
    Independent and bright
    A light in the dark.

Each spirit or soul,
    Or essence of life,
    Whether 'tis one, or all
    The living force strives -

So, to understand
    This sentient force,
    This spark, spirit of life,
    What, why, where, its source?

So, To Their Retreat

Bats in the belfry
Birds in the loft,
    Mice in the pantry
    Folk in the croft.

Children in the schoolhouse
Keepers in their shops,
    Workers in the factories
    Gardeners on plots.

Porters in stations
Shoppers in malls,
    Milkman in dairies
    Mayors in halls.

Farmers within their barns
Cattle in the sheds,
    Soldiers in barracks
    Dogs upon their beds.

So, to their retreat
    All that lead and are led.

Mischief Was His Name

Mischief was his name
    An independent cat,
With a strong clear voice
    And he'd let you know that.

White he was of coat
    A snowball of a cat,
Who sharpen'd his claws
    On the carpet and mat.

Always on the prowl
    In garden or in field,
'Til one summer's day
    On the lane, he was killed.

By a car he died,
    For he never did learn,
Getting in the way,
    Across your path would turn.

No more will he prowl
    The garden and the field,
We miss him so much
    Now his voice is stilled.

Mask of Life

The mask of life
    Hides still, to confound
Secrets of time,
    Which are so profound.

For each species
    That lives on our earth,
Each animal
    Bird, all that have worth –

All have a mask
    Behind which they hide,
Man has his mask
    And few can confide.

Nature herself
    In all her glory,
Masks each season
    As fits the story.

Flies Now the Spirit

Flies now the spirit
    Amongst the wide spaces,
Forever seeking
    Hidden truth, time embraces.

With empathy felt,
    Understand creations
Forms and interplay,
    Subtle implications.

Acknowledging fear
    From whatsoever the source,
Primeval of thought
    Action, or nature's course.

Then seek the beauty
    In the sights and the sounds,
Of life around us
    So sublime, yet abounds.

Thus flies the spirit
    Wherever it will seek,
Even to the stars
    And the spaces they keep.

Flies High the Flag

Old England flies high the flag
In this year of twenty-twelve,
    Holding the Olympic Games
    Began by strike of a bell.

Held true, the spirit of games
In all their diverse forms,
    Many a medal of gold
    Silver and bronze were worn.

Uplifting the atmosphere
With glee and shouts of triumph,
    As the athletes reach their peak
    Advancing athletic science.

So at last the final day
The closing ceremony,
    For all those who took part were
    The best in humanity.

Quicker By Far

As swift as the wind
    Time passes on by,
As fleet as a hawk
    On the hunt does fly.

From child to adult
    Seems just a few years,
Then 'tis middle age
    Just months it appears.

Then quicker by far
    Than all of past time,
Suddenly become
    With the showing signs –

One of the aged,
    Known as elderly,
And you wonder if
    A conspiracy –

Had taken your years,
    And you're wearily
Left to fight your fears,
    Leaving memory.

Veil of Secrecy

The mind, hidden behind
    A living shadow'd curtain,
In secret, defines
    And perceives the uncertain.

All that is mystery,
    Hidden, is lost or unknown
The mind grapples and grasps
    With fingers of thought, alone.

Seeking always to see
    That which the mind does not see,
For the mind never sleeps
    Behind its veil of secrecy.

The Haunting Winds

The winds that rise and fall
    Upon the living earth,
Arise from where they're born
    In mysterious birth.

They roam the world at will
    Gentle as a whisper,
Or violent in anger
    Where none can resist her.

Wind is like a woman
    Can be soft and feline,
Or spit with such temper
    When aroused or inclined.

So does the spirit move
    In a breeze or gale shown
What haunts the atmosphere
    With such emotion sown.

What aches, what tenderness
    What savagery felt
Within winds so to haunt,
    That we unknowing, are dealt.

Truth

When the spirit flies
    To those open spaces,
Delving, seeking truth
    Amid nature's graces.

It will find itself
    Alone, yet touching life's
Own elemental
    Pulse, all nature comprise.

From wild meadowsweet
    To the largest tall tree,
From pine topp'd mountain
    To the deepest blue sea.

Or mouse to a man
    Mud hut to a city,
The spirit discerns
    Compassion and pity.

Yet flies still, beyond,
    Pass'd the pearl-white moon's stare
Pass'd the sun and on to
    Truth, the spirit can share.

Where the Spirit Has Trod

The soft glow of twilight
    Fades into the shadows
    And they, fast become night's
        Veil o'er town and meadow.

Within the summer sky
    The gems of darkness grow,
    Like glittering spangles
        Bright as diamonds show.

While fingers of a breeze
    Gently caress the face,
    Like a secret whisper
        A touch of nature's grace.

Filling the warm night air
    The smell and scent arise,
    Of sweet honeysuckle
        And garden rose to lie –

Upon awaken'd senses
    Where the spirit has trod,
    Touching the heart and mind
        P'chance a gift, from the Gods.

The Wildest Field-Green

They reach their long fingers
    Do brambles in hedges,
Ever thrusting their life
    Probing to the edges.
As they snake and entwine
    Through the wildest field-green,
And their weapons of thorn
    Are aggressive and mean.

They can quite overrun,
    Overwhelm the poor hedge,
All because of their strength
    Overcoming all veg'.
Yet come early autumn
    Shows the bramble has grace,
From clusters of blossom
    Comes a fruit of sweet taste.

All at Once

The painters are here,
    Painting the exterior
Of our country house,
    With ladders extended are
Busy with their brushes
    Tape and paint with flare,
While the gardener
    De-heads the dead roses,
Weeds and mows the lawns
    Tending all that grows, he is.
All the while the cleaners
    Are cleaning every room,
With the raucous song
    Of the vacuum's tune.
The smell of polish
    Where dashing dusters flit,
One doesn't know where
    To turn, or go, or sit,
Why do things happen
    All at once? Why is it?

Sky and Garden Green

Release the spirit to rise
    Sending the mind up high,
To roam, seek and enjoy
    The blue-bright summer sky.

Or on wing, swoop to where
    The hot-light of the sun
Embraces all the land,
    Through summer-hours to come.

Butterfly, bee and beetle
    Flit and run as they will,
Amongst the garden-green
    Their appetites to fill.

While the scents of grasses
    Bloom and heady flower,
Reaches now the senses
    Proclaiming summer's power.

Secrets Lost

Below the garden lawn
    Runs an ancient stream.
Said to carry energy
    Mysteries, unseen.

Ten thousand years or more
    Their strangeness had been known.
A stream amongst many
    Where a ley-line was shown.

Stream and ley-line converge
    To places of power,
Denoting a hill-fort
    Or early church tower.

Once we knew the secret
    Of these energy lines,
Now that secret is lost
    Through the passing of time.

The Receiving Mind

Welcome to life today,
    With its raucous diverse sounds,
    That fall upon the ear,
    And each of us does surround.

Such sights and sounds impact
    Upon the receiving mind,
    As cities' multitudes
    Do hurry against the time.

The harsh sounds of traffic
    And screech of aircraft engines.
    Together with sirens
    From vehicles attending.

All backed by a scene
    Of multi-coloured lights,
    Advertisement posters
    And more, a myriad sights.

With the ever-sounding
    Beat of rock music, relayed
    Through small radios,
    And all, do irritate.

We, Tree, Field and Flower

Even the trees are wilting
    In this hot humid air.
Awaiting a fall of rain
    That all of life can share.

The summer's heat is sultry
    Heavy and oppressive,
It bears down on the spirit
    And is too excessive.

So we wait for cooling winds
    We, tree, field and flower,
And the relief that it brings
    With a fresh sweet shower.

There are times when our climate
    Becomes unbearable,
Yet the passing years have shown
    It's unpredictable.

A Constant State of Flux

There is no solid foundation,
No long term reality
Exists for human endeavour,
    In all totality.

Whether it be our inventions,
Towns, or cities, the crux
For all mankind's creations
    Is the constant state of flux.

Thus what is now new and wonderful
Is quickly outdated,
Or be it a new-style building
    A short life is fated.

Our technology and buildings
Will not last a thousand years,
We live in a fast changing world
    That reflects man's joy and fears.

A Million Gods?

What universal energies
    Manipulate reality,
As if, in interpretation
    Perchance are like humanity.

Energies of power and thought
    Pervading all, yet so distant,
With god-like powers determine
    Humanities own existence.

Both creative and destructive,
    Multitudinous worlds and suns,
With such diverse creatures and minds
    Are born and die over aeons.

So are there a million gods
    For millions of the latter?
Or pure creative energy
    Forming and transforming matter?

Their Spirit Travels On

Where does all that life go?
All those souls who lived before,
    Especially those with talent
    Above the base did soar.

Where is the freed spirit
Of those so advanced to gain?
    Or the discoverers who stopp'd
    Cruel illness and pain?

Where the music masters
And their beautiful melodies?
    That stirred humanity's soul
    The heart in sympathy.

Just where is all that life
That once did live and beat so strong?
    Wherever they are or become
    Their spirit travels on.

The Last Dance

Summer slowly closes as
    The year approaches autumn,
The long hot days are changing
    And the hours begin to shorten.

For with the cooling weather
    Begins the last carefree dance,
Of nature's green and colour
    Field, meadow and garden plants.

Now with the strengthening breeze
    Sees the trees begin to sway,
With diversity of leaf
    Moved to dance through the day.

So on into the autumn
    Yet, before cold winter's scene,
The winds softly bring about
    Summer's last dance, serene.

Washing the Dust Away

Such a thunderous downpour
    Upon the hot dry land,
Creating running rivers
    And riverlets that ran –

Down road, lane and track
    Washing the dust away,
Freshening the countryside
    And sweetening the day.

Cooling the still summer air
    And bathing all beneath
The sullen, storm-wrought dark clouds,
    Lightning and thunder wreath'd.

'Til the washed dripping land
    Emerged from the curtain
Of such a fall of water,
    Where all of thirst did gain.

Cottage, Meadow and Hedges of May

    Reflected sunlight
        From the hilltop cottage,
    Gleams through the treetops
        From its bright cream image –

That beyond the hedge
    In all majesty stands,
As it has long stood
    Through the years, on the land.

Before the broad hedge
    Lies the old rich meadow,
Once home and succour
    Grass and hay of yellow.

Where ponies did graze
    And spend the summer day,
With cottage, meadow
    And the hedges of may.

Shadow'd and bordered
    By the tall shading trees,
Enclosing the view
    Like a picture, one sees.

Cloudscape

A mackerel sky
    In a sea of air,
Full patten marked
    Which the clouds did share.

Bright-lit from above
    By a ghost-white moon,
While spread far beyond
    Shone stars of pale-blue.

Across the night sky
    Ev'ry cloudlet there,
Became by design
    A cloudscape full rare.

Like Sun, Like Song

As wind and rain,
    Like sun, like song,
Or day, or night,
    life carries on.

For the high-born
    And the low-born,
Others between
    Whichever form –

Humanity takes,
    Animals, birds,
Fauna and green
    They all confer –

Their true essence
    Upon the earth,
Thus they do take
    And give their worth.

True to being
    Of spirit sought,
Pervading all
    The world has wrought.

Beauty of the Land

As seen from a distance
    The land is so tranquil.
Whatever the season
    Beauty is revealed.

Which one of the seasons
    Has a merit beyond,
Spring, summer, or autumn?
    Or winter, cold and long?

Each is as picturesque
    Dressed as nature may,
The choice is yours to make
    From spring to Christmas Day.

Yet within field or wood
    If in the midst you stand,
You see such perfection
    When you're close to the land.

As August Becomes September

As September follows August
Dragonflies dart here and there,
While wayside fruiting hedgerows scent
    The late warm, still summer air.

That finds the dog and cat asleep
Lying on the garden lawn,
Far too tired to run about
    Looking now, so very worn.

Bloom and blossoms begin to droop
For they need a little rain,
Even the houseflies seem tired
    Resting on the window pane.

Slowly the sun travels the day
And the shadows silent creep,
As August becomes September
    With its bounty, fresh and sweet.

A Delicate Balance

All that was and all that is
    Together with all that will be,
    Is a delicate balance
    In the hands of humanity.

A wrong word at the wrong time,
    Or a sudden move unprovok'd,
    Could strike a dangerous spark
    In a world where fear is stoked.

Where trust is worn to a thread
    And old friends become suspicious,
    Our earthly nations reveal
    They are still very malicious.

Will we learn to overcome
    Our strong and primitive nature?
    Or by fault tip the balance
    Of what is, stealing the future.

Expectation

The sky is one,
    One colour, wall to wall,
Insipid grey
    Dull of light overall.

Comes September
    With such a dreary day,
Expectation
    Dampened, now to lay –

Heavy on the mind
    For September the first,
Is not to shine
    In warm light, but converse.

Last of summer
    Beginning of Autumn,
The mellow month
    Whether grey or warm sun.

On Silent Wings

Shadows from drifting cloud
    Wrought upon the moonlit night,
Softly cloak all that's seen
    By the pale silvery light.

As if on silent wings
    Each passing cloud stole by,
Releasing light once more
    To illuminate the sky –

In age-old mystery
    Full borne upon lands below,
Cold moonlight bathes all
    In a haunting ghost-like glow.

Ghostly or lovers light?
    Whatever the attraction,
The moon's many faces
    Holds still, such fascination.

Life's Thorns

Beware of life they say
From the moment you are born,
You are susceptible
    For it comes with many thorns.

As you travel through life
You will find them ev'ry day,
Wherever you may turn
    There is a thorn in your way.

Whether its position
Or you find you lack money,
You can bet there's a thorn
    Just making your life crummy.

Even when successful
You will always find a thorn,
Hidden behind something
    That must now be found and drawn.

Neither One

Spiders webs strung ev'rywhere
    Shining bright with dew,
Spiders hiding out of sight
    For that's what spiders do.

Meadows green and cultured lawns
    Vehicles in the drive,
All show the changing month
    For all are covered, far and wide –

In night-time's fall of dew,
    That in itself, expresses
A change within old nature's
    Many forms and dresses.

Sparkling webs, glistening lawns
    A summer or autumn sun?
The weather may be changing
    Yet is still, neither one.

Upon Summer Warmth

I watch the insects flying free
    Around the garden they share,
The bees that seek the flowers
    Butterflies wings near' light as air –

That flutter by so silently
    Lifted upon summer warmth,
To erratic fly here, there,
    Each so diverse of colour wrought.

They settle to take the nectar
    From each bright flowering head,
Flitting to the next in haste
    As we with summer wine are fed.

Transient Spirit

Is there a transient spirit
    That pervades the universe?
A spiritual energy
    Opposite bad and perverse.

A natural calming power
    Within ev'ry particle,
The great clouds of galactic dust
    Sun, planet and chemical.

Perhaps 'tis theory, quite unknown?
    Yet perchance this could exist,
Unknown throughout all time and space
    Undetected, yet does persist.

Creating all nature's beauty
    Wherever it may be found,
A spirit that's in you and me
    And all good things, tightly bound.

Good Intentions

As one gets older
One loses patience,
Yet more compassionate
    And not so complacent.

The older one gets
The more sensitive
And sentimental you are.
    Tenderness is relative –

Relative to age,
Sensitivity
And thoughtful understanding
    Of vulnerability.

With all these feelings
Thus far mentioned,
One can easily become
    Captive to good intentions.

Alone In a Field

From where I sit, I see
    A young girl walking
Slowly through the tall grass,
    Nature consorting –

In an unkempt field of
    Wild grass and hemlock,
Cow parsley, sowthistles,
    Hedge shaded burdock.

With other wild flowers
    Part hidden from sight,
Buttercup and speedwell
    Dandelion bright.

Oft' stooping to gather
    The gifts that appealed,
She wandered through nature
    Alone in a field.

Air, House and Fen

The fan works overtime
In the writer's den,
As the sun heats up the air
    The house and the fen.

Where a myriad flies
Appear and annoy,
Settling and buzzing
    Their usual ploy.

Micro irritations
Are everywhere,
Walking about your desk
    Or landing in your hair.

Then come the drunken wasps
Looking for trouble,
As sounding like band-saws
    They fall and tumble –

Down to join the flies and
Unsteadily land
On desk, or page and floor
    Wind-blown by the fan.

In Secrecy

Where are those shining disks?
    That travel silently
Across our wide blue skies
    In unknown secrecy.

Appearing here and there
    In ones, twos, sometimes more,
Of such diverse design
    Can at speed, dip and soar.

What is their strange purpose?
    Their final objective?
For they have been with us
    Through time, long connected.

Their place or origin
    Is still yet to be known,
Yet one day we'll know the truth
    When in stature, are grown.

Imagination

Imagination runs
    With thoughts of every kind,
As thinking will permit
    Such diverse answers to find.

Dependent each upon
    The mind so to plunder,
Thus to interpretate
    Each mysterious wonder.

What imagination
    Or great truths to decipher?
So many swift arrows
    Consciously loos'd to fly there –

In search of those answers
    Most complex, that so evade
Their capture and remain
    Still, in darkness and shade.

To Mellow Close

The summer sprites
  Are leaving,
Autumn spirit
  Is weaving –

Further between
  The seasons,
To mellow close
  And ease on –

To winter's freeze,
  Blending all
In dormant sleep
  Through ice 'n' squall.

Day After Day

The sun comes up, then sinks down
Day after day after day,
Illuminating bright the world
    Then suddenly goes away.

Forever changing night and day,
All because of our planet,
Its spinning motion is too fast
    Spun as if by a magnet.

Held in space by forces of mass
Cannot deviate its path,
Never to lengthen or shorten
    Night's shadows or daylight cast.

So we experience the sunlight
As we turn around the sun,
Then once again in darkness bound
    As on we spin to kingdom come.

Old Laws and New

With thoughts of ages
    And all they imply,
The immensity
    Of history that lies –

In years long past
    Creating the how,
For all who live
    In old England now.

What of those days
    That made England strong,
Is it to be
    The nation's new song?

From such dither
    And weakness spring forth
A strong people,
    Who shall so endorse –

Old laws and new
    That these thoughts persist,
Thus for those to come,
    Mercy and justice.

Fruit, Leaf and Bloom

The trees bow low
    With the season's growth,
Each leafy branch dips
    Touching plants below.

For now September
    Reigns, mellow and cool,
Yet still golden warmth
    Can ignite and befool –

Nature's denizens
    To brightly parade,
Their fruit, leaf and bloom
    Each before they fade –

In the cold dark months
    That slowly encroach,
While rich autumn glows
    Linger, beyond reproach.

As a Gift

I have seen the beauty
That the world has to offer,
I have not seen it all
      But know, green lands are softer.

I have seen the mountains
Awe-inspiring majesty,
The valleys, lakes, rivers
      And wild vistas one can see.

Yet it's in old England's
Picturesque meadows and hills,
Villages and woodlands
      That beauty is fulfilled.

The very nature speaks
Of the land and folk alike,
A gentleness given
      That warms, as a gift from life.

Just a Few

Bird and bee
Rabbit and flea,
Dog and cat
Chicken and rat,
Just a few
From nature true,
Of the life
That run and fly,
Underground
Or above found,
In earth 'n' air
We all do share,
Without these
Life could not be,
For earth, read
    Catastrophe.

To Reason

Within the confines of one's mind
    To reason about life,
To think upon mysteries
    Violence and world strife –

We come upon the ultimate
    That halts such probing thoughts,
For the world and thus its knowledge
    Cannot for all its faults –

Its evolving histories
    Be so unravelled,
By any discerning mind
    However widely travelled.

So to each who seek for the truth
    Wisdom in part is found,
We cannot accept such knowledge
    Yet, for earth's secrets profound.

Fingers of Life

The fingers of life claw the air
    In erratic movement,
Searching, reaching, feeling
    With primordial intent,
Amidst the many forms
    Newly sprung from the earth,
Living cells so diverse
    In a convulsive surge,
That wriggle and struggle
    And reach to extend,
Their thin tenuous limbs
    As spreading roots descend.
While small furry creatures
    Just the first of a kind,
Scamper for rich berries
    And such food as they find.
The seeking green tendrils
    Along with small creatures,
Are the fingers of life,
    The first, of the future.

Golden Days

The gentle breeze of summer
To stronger winds become,
These in turn to gale-force blow
    And cold replaces sun.

As autumn slowly passes
'Tis always with regret,
To see the last golden days
    Give way to cloud and wet.

So into winter's darkness
Frost and icy weather,
We slowly are immersed
    With hide, fur and feather.

Under winter's coverlet
No sun or warmth discern,
Thus we wait the dark months out
    'Til golden days return.

Chimneys of the Shire

I see the country villages
    In the lowlands and on high,
By field and woodland green
    And tall oaks against the sky.

I see the smoke from chimneys
    Drifting over the shire,
Sweet wood-smoke, perfuming air
    From each warm friendly fire.

Where ere an aged cottage
    Sends forth its smoke from chimneys,
Recalling a countryside
    Picturesque and whimsey.

Once part of old England
    Were the chimneys of the shire,
Now such a rarity found
    Is the smoke from friendly fires.

This Colourful Land

As if painted yellow
    The fields softly lie,
With their hedges of green
    Under autumn skies.

Sleepily, the lands drift
    Towards winter's rest.
While the cloud-softened light
    Lays, as to caress –

This bountiful season,
    Of bronze, gold, yellow,
Colours rich to the eye
    Mature and mellow –

And we, who move upon
    This colourful land
Also to autumn brought,
    Wrought by the same hand.

Spider Town

I no longer own
    The garden shed,
It's been colonised
    Restructured by webs.

It's now, Spider Town
    For many types
Of diverse colour
    Plain, spots and stripes.

Small and large abide
    In grey web-homes,
Tunnel-webs low down
    Mid pots and gnomes.

The bigger spiders
    Weave wide grey veils,
From whence they await
    What prey thus hales.

Webs and strands, strung
    Sticky and thick,
A real Spider Town
    In my shed, sits.

Bramble, Elder and Apple

So lays the bramble
    The elder and apple,
Those wild of the field
    With hedge rose that settles.
Tangled together
    Thorn sharp, interwoven,
The living border
    'Twixt field 'n' meadow grown.
Now quiet they lay
    Energy expended,
Spring and summer life
    At rest as intended.
The season closes
    Upon all nature's lands,
Except for such life
    Winter planted by man.
So lays the hedgerow
    The elder and apple,
Bright rose that clings
    Together with bramble.

Somewhere, Sometime

And does the spirit fly
    On wings of spirit borne?
Perchance then when we die,
    Or more could be the norm!

Does it fly where others
    To a netherworld go?
Or is it natural
    For energy to roam?

Perhaps to other realms
    We are so swiftly drawn,
Thus in new dimensions
    We need not, old life forms.

Do spirits die again
    Becoming what other?
Or are we absorbed
    In primordial matter?

Yet, the cycle will turn
    Again creating thought,
Somewhere, sometime, to life
    The spirit will be brought.

As If Upon an Ark

Through the window of my room
    In daylight and in dark,
I see time fast sliding by
    As if upon an ark.

Each day followed by the night
    For first in turn, the sun,
Chas'd by the moon and stars
    As round and round they run.

Expressing the urgency
    Of life so quickly liv'd,
For each animal and man
    And all that is conceiv'd.

Days and nights run into years
    And the years turn like days,
Thus time holds the greatest fear
    As it rushes away.

The Reason Why

Does any man know where
    He's going in this life
From whence he thus has come,
    Or know the reason why?

What is the real purpose
    Of us all, being here?
As sentient beings
    Prone to ills and fear.

Is there some real purpose
    A universal task,
We'll be called upon
    To do amongst the stars?

Or are we here by fault?
    Perhaps an accident?
Unrelated to plan
    Risen from rich sediment.

Humanity

It makes one pause
    And to deeply think,
We are so small
    A connecting link,
In the long chain
    Of man's history,
Link after link
    Wrought humanity.
From the first birth
    Down through the ages,
Coupling each link
    To the next, brought sages,
Who taught such truths
    As wisdom allowed.
So did we learn
    Becoming a crowd,
It makes one pause
    And to deeply think
We are as strong
    As the weakest link.

The Breath

There is such a blast
    Coming from the west,
It's bending all the trees
    With such spirited zest.

Rattling the gate
    Moaning through rafters,
Blowing the loose chaff
    Still faster and faster.

Clouds slide silently
    Dull grey through the sky,
While below, such a draught
    Exceeding strong, does ply.

This wind that does blow,
    This natural force,
Is just simply the breath
    Of the air, from its source.

Nature's Daughters

To walk the lane together,
    Tread the meadows green,
Ramble through the woodlands
    Joyful and serene.

Then stride the pine-clad hills,
    Rich in scented air,
Walk the stream-fed valleys
    Which cottage and river share.

Or climb the reaching mountains
    Thrusting darkly high,
With cloud covered summits
    Hidden in the sky.

Perhaps to drift in silence
    Upon calm waters,
Lost in dreamlike thoughts
    Amidst nature's daughters.

Both High and Low

So simple a growth of life,
    So basic a shoot,
As a multitude spread
    Tenacious of root.

So common to the sight
    Softening the land,
Ever reproducing
    By nature's wild hand.

Such a plant, unjustly
    Ignored, unseen,
Yet, cultured by some
    For fineness of green.

With colour it covers
    Wayside and meadow,
And grows in all places
    Both high and the low.

So unnoticed in life
    Is the green of grass,
Giving beauty to the eye
    And nurture to last.

September's Face

September's the month
    To search for the prize,
Prize of wild mushrooms
    That grow large in size.

There's button and cup
    And horse mushrooms white,
Pushing their heads through
    The loam to the light.

Just after dawn will
    See them arrayed
In meadow and field
    Fresh sprung for the day.

A prize from the fields
    In looks and in taste,
These mushrooms all white
    September's wild face.

The Indulgent Spirit

To drift high above the earth,
    To lose oneself 'twixt light and dark,
Higher than the floating clouds
    Above the swallow and the lark.

In such dreamlike essence
    Cast by the indulgent spirit,
To overcome such ties
    As the mind strongly exhibits.

To cut the chains that bind
    Us, to crude earth's reality,
And let loose the longing
    That is now in captivity.

Freeing the mind to soar
    To diverse realms on high,
Could change the very state
    Of awareness, the very life.

Season to Season

The ponies graze in sunlit meadows,
    While bordering trees and hedges
Rustle and move in the playful wind,
    Yet, at end of season pledges
The return of much colder weather
    Where summer skies of blue fast fade,
Replaced by a heavy curtain
    Which upon the land so darkly lays.

So ends the season and warmer climes
    The last fruits of hedgerow and field,
And the charm of birdsong is stilled
    Over meadow, valley and weald.
Old winter once more will change the land
    Where most to sleep and rest will fall,
Until again there will be skies of blue
    And sweet of song, the birds will call.

The Roads of England

The roads of England are
    Not wide or long enough,
To take modern traffic
    Fast, you just cannot rush.

At first our roads were laid
    By Roman engineers,
And little did they change
    For many many years.

And thus the routes we take
    Are upon age-old lanes,
Modernised with asphalt
    But still are near the same.

Therefore what then to plan
    To lay vast tracks of road?
Or pass a law to ban
    Vehicles, light of load?

Turn to peddle power,
    Short urban electric?
Or on wing learn to fly
    That might do the trick?

Half a Laugh and Half a Tear

With half a pie
    And half a beer,
With half a laugh
    And half a tear.
The old man sat
    Alone, hidden,
In a corner
    And unbidden,
Either body
    Or by spirit,
That the inn's old
    Age did give it,
So many years
    So many thoughts,
Gone were the friends
    The love, once sought.
Each memory
    Caught and fast lost,
Alone he sat
    Not without cost,
With half a pie
    And half a beer,
With half a laugh
    And half a tear.

When Clouds

Sometimes English weather
    Un-beckoned and unsought,
Can fall upon the land
    And we are quickly caught.

Whether we want or not
    To have a drenching bath,
We get it just the same
    When clouds, their waters cast –

And all beneath are soaked,
    Although we need the rain
It seems to fall on us
    To cause the greatest bane.

It floods roads and rivers
    Creating lakes in fields,
Everything is damp
    Which causes sniffs and chills.

Why can't it rain at night?
    Leaving days warm and dry,
Then we could plan our lives
    Not gazing at the sky.

A World of Thought

Eight billion worlds
    Upon a world,
Eight billion souls
    A mix of pearls,
That shine bright or dull
    Dependent on,
Creation's rare gift
    From parents, born.
Yet each a world true
    Unto itself,
A living spirit
    Separate, felt,
A single life form
    A world of thought,
That intermingles
    With all, that's sought.
Thus, is just a part,
    A tiny world,
Turning amongst worlds
    Of life, unfurl'd.

A World of Light

Within a world of light
    My world was incandescent,
Now the world has changed
    And lights are now fluorescent.

There is also neon
    And there's argon gas as well,
Replacing mercury
    A vapour of green, to tell.

We've also L E Ds
    Bright little sparks are to hand,
Many lights to see by
    When darkness falls on the land.

Yet, still the humble bulb
    With it's fine thin filament,
Is still with us today
    A part of life's endearment.

Upon Two Legs

It stood upon a shelf
    In the garden shed,
Like a woodland elf
    Awaiting to be fed.

What kind of creature
    With pointed ears and tail,
Stands upon two legs
    Whether hide, fur or scale.

In its little hands
    It held a fallen nut,
Turning it about
    Chattering with its luck.

With his find held tight
    Between its small sharp teeth,
It scrambled away
    On such fast furry feet.

A flick of its tail
    And with a bounding run,
The squirrel took flight
    For the shed, it did shun.

Bedroom Bears

Upon the bedroom shelves
    They sit in ones and pairs,
Rich in diverse colour
    Are these soft teddy-bears.

Some have colourful hats
    Others a woolly scarf,
One has a baby bear
    Collected from the past.

They sit and look at me
    And I look back at them,
Each time I go to bed
    Around the hour of ten.

They are a part of me
    In a silly sort of way,
For all that I do own
    In silence, seem to say –

We are you, you are we,
    And here, in ones and pairs
We sit contentedly,
    Just bedroom teddy-bears.

On This Earth

Why this planet?
    This earth of ours?
What's so special?
    What empowers
Such decisions
    Of life and mind?
So selected
    To place and time.
Thus to be born
    On this earth, here,
And not upon
    A distant sphere,
Some unknown world
    Light years away,
Alien born
    To stranger days,
Yet, life placed me
    Here on this earth,
And so should prove
    We are of worth.

Meadow Home

Where have all the rabbits gone?
    I haven't seen one,
I used to see the meadow
    Lit by summer sun,
And playing there, young rabbits
    So oblivious
To all, outside their small world,
    Their patch, green and lush,
Birds still hide in the hedges
    And stalk the rich fields,
But the rabbits have vanished
    Their life now stilled.
I miss those furry creatures
    Running, gambolling,
Innocently chasing
    Each other in spring
Or lying in autumn warmth
    For now they had grown,
Whilst the youngsters were at play
    In their meadow home.

Compliance

The human race is
   Catastrophe sown
No matter the politics
   The world's history has shown.

From the privileged
   They come, most without
A sense of realism,
   And experience, have nowt.

Expensive their time
   In rich high-brow schools,
And apart from the office
   Where the pen is the main tool –

Their grip of England's
   Day to day living,
Heeds not her powers and needs
   But compliance and giving.

In Secrecy

See the mists, low lying,
    Obscuring the ground
Like a veil laid, flowing,
    Mystically found.

Tree and hedge, fence and gate
    Emerge from below,
Rising above the vapour
    Which so ghostly flows.

Thus, lost in a cloudlike
    Land, partly unseen,
Quiet, so faint of sound
    As if in a dream.

An artistic painting
    Caught in mystery,
This October morning
    Wrought in secrecy.

When We Were Young

I knew a girl
    Many years ago,
When we were young
    And time was slow.
A girl of looks
    And her name was Jane,
Living quite close
    Down Sycamore Lane.
Gold hair in curl
    With eyes of bright green,
Slender of form
    Like a beauty queen.
One day we fought
    Over a trifle,
So we did part
    In pain, regretful.
Yet, soon did find
    A girl who was true
With hair of gold
    And eyes of blue.

Secret Dreams

Thus the mind does reach
    And the spirit flies,
Out, out, out and there
    Upon a moonbeam rides.

To where dark spaces
    Are lit by starlight,
And the circling moons
    Beaming face is full bright.

There upon the wash
    Of darkened spaces,
Full-fae the light is
    Where the heart embraces.

To fly in silence
    Upon pale moonbeams,
The spirit to seek
    Those hidden secret dreams.

A Servant of Time

Today I realised
After a lifetime's living,
I had reached the stage where
    Life was no longer thrilling.

I lived the years of youth,
With their early adventures,
Courted beautiful women
    Labours of love remembered.

Now upon this plain of age
Stand and view reality,
The past, present and future
    Are wrought with finality.

Whatever year, time or age
Befalls the living spirit,
It is then, for our journey
    No matter how you wish it.

A journey that rushes by
And so, here upon this plain,
I stand, a servant of time,
    Awaiting the call by name.

Born In Nature's Lair

The breath of life flows
    To softly caress,
Each spirit of life
    That moves or rests.

Plant and fauna, all
    Upon the landscape,
Rustle, bow and nod
    And so they relate –

To the breath of life,
    The cloud-bearing air,
Wherein each fresh breeze
    Born in nature's lair –

Washes and freshens
    Giving all such life,
Thus touching all things
    Each day and each night.

Verdant Green

To live within the countryside
    You live amongst the verdant green,
And in comparison you are
    No bigger than a plant it seems.

For true reality deflates
    The ego of the brash human mind,
Reducing down to what you are,
    Very small, both in size and kind.

Nature has so many faces
    So many exquisite life forms,
We, as intelligent creatures
    Should understand, all that is born –

Has a part to play, a balance
    That sustains such a landscape seen,
Large or small, all are of this land
    This countryside of verdant green.

Elkie, a Friend

I lost a friend today
    A loyal friend and true,
Companion through the years
    While my love for her grew.

A black and tan coated
    German shepherd, female,
With soft brown friendly eyes
    And a long sweeping tail.

I met her one spring day
    When down and so alone,
Becoming my partner
    For both in trust had grown.

A very gentle dog
    So friendly and sincere,
She was part of my life
    With her presence, so dear.

No more will she sit
    Under the willow tree,
Running to chase the birds
    Or be a friend to me –

For her spirit has flown
    Leaving me so bereft,
She was a joy to own
    And now, she sleeps at rest.

Borne on Time's Wings

In life there is death,
Death is part of life,
Is life a part of death?
    A different kind of life?
Or is there nothing more?
The conscious mind dies
And nothingness remains
    When we in earth do lie.
Yet, the body is only
A vehicle to hold
Each energised spirit's
    Sentient spark's true role.
To be aware of all
That time wrought, on earth.
To become one with them
    In knowledge and re-birth.
A re-birth that perchance
Will carry the spirit
Across the universe,
    Borne on time's wings, complicit –
With all in reality,
And beyond this realm
With such understanding,
    As if at a god-like helm.

In Full Worth

When love and beauty cease
To be a part of life,
Creature, plant or human
    Cut off, as with a knife.
No matter which or why
There remains a sad loss,
Of spirit and living
    A goodness we have lost.
Be it beauty or strength
Of mind, as in friendship,
Faithfulness and courage
    Are all true heartfelt gifts.
The colour of a bloom
The perfume of a rose,
A graceful standing tree
    And all of green that grows
Our feathered friends in flight
Nature's little creatures,
The cat by the fire
    A dog's defined features.
Our love of all these things
That we share on this earth,
Is given back to us
    In spirit and full worth.

Companions

I have two new
    Motorised gizmos,
They're everywhere at once
    Or to me seem to be so.

Two small puppies
    Which are just two months old,
Both black and tan in colour
    And for their age, are quite bold.

German shepherds
    Full of rough and tumble,
A devoted faithful breed
    Guardians of the humble.

They're boisterous
    And very playful dogs,
Leaving a lot of teeth-marks
    On hands, furniture and logs.

Noisy sounding
    From early morn 'til late,
But I love these young puppies
    For the companions they make.

Of Thought

Reality or religion,
    Myth, mystic or normality,
Ancient and modern
    We all must learn to see!

No matter which former or creed
    Philosophy, history taught,
All become a question
    Of thinking and of thought.

Defining all that is in space
    Matter and energy wrought,
The coming together
    Of atoms should have taught –

The matrix of matter and life
    Formed by coincidence,
Perhaps by accident
    Seems to make much more sense –

For reality will find a
    Balance for all things persisting,
No matter length of time
    Primordial knitting.

October 31st

Tonight the thirty-first of October
    The night of Halloween
A celebrated historic event
    Wrought from a bygone scene.

Cruel and fearful were those ancient times
    Stirred by wicked liars
For reasons of greed or of jealously
    Put to stake and fire –

Innocent women of those simple days
    For heresy and wild lies,
Brought about through the Church and its sad priests
    Who should have been more wise.

Now from those long ago days of horror
    We have our Halloween,
Of witches and ugly masks to frighten
    And make our children scream.

As a Seed

Man is like a living ear
    Of ripening golden corn,
That's sown in fertile soil
    To grow in summer warmth.

Each ear a separate seed
    Upon the life-giving straw,
Standing tall side by side
    Growing by nature's law.

When at last the ears ripen
    And the corn is harvested,
The seeds are thus taken
    To be the heart of bread.

Leaving just a dying stalk
    And the husk that once grew,
As a protective coat
    For the seed it once knew.

The True Dawn

When, in times ages
    Mankind sees the light,
Not only in mind but deed
    Then, will he rise sure and bright –

In the enlighten'd
    Glow of the true dawn,
Whereby humanity steps
    Beyond young minds, newly born,
To enter god-like
    Into the cosmos,
With greater understanding
    Of life, order and chaos.

Thereby rightfully
    Fulfilling mankind's
Destiny in creations
    Never-ending grand design.

The Father of Them All

The biggest deceivers of all
    Are the days, months and years,
That come and swiftly pass on by
    Leaving both joy and tears.

For so quickly do they arrive
    And just as quickly gone,
Fleeting light and shadow as the
    Spirit of life looks on.

But, the greatest of deceivers
    Is the father of them all,
And rules all our realities
    By times wrought halls.

So Precarious

Come reality of life,
    So precarious
Is your existence,
    Unpredictable or worse.
Changing weather cycles,
    Your extremes of nature,
Unbidden rise of seas
    All is such danger.

The earth is susceptible
    From internal extremes,
Likewise from spatial depths
    Come radiation streams.
Or hurtling from hidden paths
    Are the rocks of ages,
Life is so precarious
    Without our human rages.

Topaz and Diamond

Wish upon the sunlit glitter
    Of an ice-white frost-covered morn,
That perchance this fairyland
    Once more in magic shall dawn.

Trees of bright crystalline white
    Above meadows diamond bright,
While sugar-glazed streams reflect
    All, in their hoar-frost light.

Clear skies of the palest blue
    Ride high over this picture, keen,
Topaz and diamond together
    Colour this morning's scene.

Celebrated Season

Once more we celebrate
    This traditional day of days,
As we have so many times
    Where snow-white lays, or grey of greys.

Unpredictable weather
    Often spoils this merry season,
So we just abide within
    Our warm abodes, with good reason.

We hibernate for these days
    Come each Christmas celebration,
Cocoon'd with Father Christmas
    Fir trees, rich fare and relations.

The give and take of presents
    Within the glow of coloured lights,
Has little to do with Christ
    And much with long-held pagan rites.

To Seek

When most of your days have gone
And each year may be your last,
Savour all that's gone before
    Whether pleasant or not, the task.
Living, spirit and body
Which in life encompasses
All that makes reality,
    As the heart now confesses.

Yet, still there is more to find,
To seek, than that which is known,
Lift your mind and send your thoughts
    Like arrows into the unknown,
Search now for that hidden truth,
The beauty of all that hides.
Beyond the far horizon
    The ultimate meaning abides.

Pickle

Pickle is a puppy
    Only three months old,
A cross between a husky
    And German shepherd bold.

He's sharp as a razor
    And fast on his feet,
He shakes all his toys about
    And isn't very neat.

His ears have stood up straight
    And he's bright of eye,
With his large round furry paws
    And tail still slim and tight.

He's learning now, nicely
    How he should behave,
To sit, to come or to stay
    To know of course, his name.

Destructive Rain

In latter years they may talk
About the constant fall of rain,
That heavily fell each day
    Forming waters to flood and lay.

First, the year when young was dry
With its date of two o twelve,
Yet soon the weather turned
    As from dark clouds, the water fell.

Flooding fields and village streets
Swelling the rivers to torrents,
To rage and so burst their banks
    Cascading wild and abhorrent.

Rushing into shops and barns
Wrecking business and movement,
Creating devastation
    And financial torment.

Bright Light

Christmas has gone,
The weather is foul,
The days are dark
    And wind does growl.

The rain never stops
Full wet and cold,
We need the sun's
    Bright light of gold.

We must endure
This loathsome weather,
And carry on
    All together –

Hoping the days
Will fast unfold,
For we need the sun's
    Bright light of gold.

Damp Days

What is this misery?
    This dark and damp life?
Rain, mist and clinging fog
    For child, man and wife.

The end of December's
    Christmas holidays,
'Twixt the twenty-fifth and
    January's rays –

Comes such dreary weather,
    Reducing the mind
And the spirit, their cheer
    At this weary time.

Until the weather turns
    To lighten our ways,
We are left in darkness
    And winter's damp days.

This Fair Day

Soft and blue the sky
This first day of January,
The sun a golden eye
    This year two o one three.

Fully commemorative
Beginning of the year,
The heart awakes to this gift
    Amidst the winter drear.

No wind disturbed the scene
And quiet pervaded all,
Except for the wild geese
    Bright of feather, loud in call –

Who settled on a field
In great numbers arrayed,
From the road they were revealed
    By Norfolk's sun this fair day.

Mists of the Mind

Such mists that cloud the mind,
    The inability to think,
Like fog on winter's day
    Obscures sight and the vital link –
With realities presence,
    Leaving the spirit quite lost
In its perception of
    Time and place, at reason's cost –
'Til such fog disperses,
    And clarity of thought returns
Awareness to the mind
    And sight, with reality.

Silent and Unseen

What mysteries abound
Upon our home, our earth?
What silent and unseen
    Entities of life lurk –

Beyond our boundaries
Or our human senses?
So lie undetected
    Leaving us defenceless –

Unable to perceive
Such alien life forms,
Or beings from our world
    Long estranged, were born –

To change over ages
Of millennium's years,
Thus, mysteries survive
    Adding to human fears.

Morning Sunlight

The morning sky has cleared
    And winter's sunlight ignites
The dew-soaked landscape,
    With sky-born flames, full bright –

Which strike each tree and barn
    Hill, dell, track and dusty lane,
While reflections dazzle
    From sun-struck window panes.

Such golden light reveals
    All the living countryside,
Cattle, sheep, field and hedge
    Church and manor, all abide –

Within the brilliant glow
    That flows, immersing the land,
As a picture fresh wrought
    From a god-like artist's hand.

White Upon White

'Tis a winter's flurry
    Through the dark night,
'Til all the cold land
    Becomes white upon white.

Then hidden black shadows
    Becomes full bright,
A new coverlet
    Brings gloom into sight.

Small crystalline snowflakes
    Floating so light,
Swirling and dancing
    As if in delight.

Fulfilling their purpose
    In winter's blight,
Painting the landscape
    In white upon white.

Song of Life

When golden dawn bursts bright and warm
    And the spirit in flight
Leaps forth, full bound in essence
    To the sweet song of life.

There to entwine the heart and soul
    With floating clouds on high,
Or rest upon soft green meadows
    And with the birds do fly.

Then languidly among flowers lie
    In perfumed harmony
With summer's singing poesy,
    As a sigh, breathlessly –

Wrought upon each tree and plant alike
    With river, lake and dell,
Mountain, wood and lonely moor
    Summer's spirit does dwell.

There

There, upon the lonely hill
    I watched the earth succumb,
Her writhing pale-lit features
    Wrought stark beneath the sun.

There, all that was good and true
    Now disregarded and destroyed,
Humanity's bright spirit
    Conveyed to the void.

There, remains now just remnants
    Of history's age-long dreams,
Crushed, along with the world
    And shall any be redeemed?

There, foresight sees far beyond
    That which is normally seen,
Will the conscience of mankind
    With unity, foresee?

For But a Moment

Within all encompassing time
There lives for but a moment,
The beauty that nature brings forth
    A gift from heaven brief sent.
Sparkling sunlight on blue waters
The rise of a harvest moon,
A flock of birds high on the wing
    Meadows with horses in June.

Bloom of a rose with sweet perfume
Woodlands on a summer's eve
Cool rivers 'twixt banks of willow
    Cornfields of gold serene.
The running murmur of a stream
A silver fish, leaping high,
Or a hedgerow's rich bloom in May
    All, but a moment of life.

So Much So Little

We know so much
    And we know so little,
Chat and expound
    Tattle and tittle.

Yet, 'tis well known
    With all our knowledge,
We are children
    In life's learned college.

As we propound
    Are propounded on,
There comes to light
    Ideas beyond
That which is known,
    And so we advance
One step at a time,
    Often thus by chance.

So we mature
    In understanding,
Yet remain bereft
    Of knowledge remaining
For us to learn,
    We must become wise
Within the sight
    Of other eyes.

All or Nothing

Why is such a saying used
    What lies behind the line?
Should one have all or nothing?
    What brings the phrase to mind?

Is it greed that empowers
    The individual
To utter such drastic measures,
    Or mouthings of a fool.

For no one should require it all
    As none should have nothing,
Depending on ability
    A little of all, must bring.

Alike are the war-maker's mind
    And the risking gambler,
A must for them the prize to gain
    Which fate or dice can render.

One does not require it all
    But needs question nothing?
Thereby we must have compromise
    Give and take in all things.

The Pages

Within life's exalted spirit
    Runs the blood of ages,
Every man, women and child
    All upon time's pages.

Animals, birds and silver fish
    As brothers related,
Upon this ancient sea-born home
    Our future care is fated.

So, with the wild earthly creatures,
    The crowning woodland trees,
Plants of land, mountain and waters
    Quiet beauty, one sees.

The spirit living in all things
    Is bound within the pages,
And is thus a part of us all
    Sap and blood of life's ages.

The Air of Life

In the year nineteen hundred
    And thirty-four, in the morn,
In September air of life
    At two a.m. I was born.

In those days preceding war
    With trolleybus and steam train,
Life was as a child could wish
    Then came the enemy planes.

Slow and hard the years went by
    'Til the tragedy ended,
Then did I begin my part
    Still young, this realm defended.

Then began the march of years
    And little did I notice,
The while, time raced on by
    Regardless of such office –

Any labours past thus wrought,
    Possessions and rewards earn'd,
Until within latter days
    Took pen to write all I'd learn'd –

Of politics and wisdom
    Stupidity and crassness,
Man's striving and endeavour
    Old history and freshness.

Beauty of the countryside
    The wonder of animals,
Trees in bloom, plants and flowers
    Fungi and all that's fruitful.

Unending whys and wherefores
    The meaning of living earth,
Such wondrous sights around us
    On this planet of our birth.

So many stories to tell
    Of people and tragedies,
With the goodness and the ills
    Peacefulness and savagery.

All such as I have noted
    In the long years since my birth,
So 'tis now I rest my pen
    In hope I have been of worth.

Part II

Light Verse

By

Elizabeth Stanley-Mallett

Previously published poems by the same author:
  Guiding Star – Forward Press, 2009
  Winter Sun – Forward Press, 2009
  Beneath Rose-Lemon Skies – Arthur H. Stockwell Ltd, 2009
  A Narrow By-Way – Anchor Books, 2010
  Valentine – Forward Press, 2010
  June Roses – Forward Press, 2010
  Little Green Men – Forward Press, 2010
  Before the Rainbow Fades Part II – Arthur H. Stockwell Ltd, 2010
  Between Night and Dancing Light Part II – Arthur H. Stockwell Ltd, 2010
  Valentine 2010 – Forward Poetry, 2011
  Three to a Seat – Forward Poetry, 2011
  Learners All – Forward Poetry, 2011
  The Door – Arthur H. Stockwell Ltd, 2011

CONTENTS

Land of Umbrellas	153
It's Just Cricket	154
Jack of All Trades	155
My Father	156
Humidity	157
Olympics	158
White Fur	159
Bonfires	160
Peas, Carrots and Taters	161
The Red Planet	162
The Dust Machine	163
Writing, Writing, Writing	164
The Village Church	165
The Deep Blue Sea	166
The Wasps	167
Where Did I Put It?	168
Butterflies	169
Celestial Bridge	170
The Boss	171
Nuts	172
Cattle Drive	173
On the Carpet	174
The Message of Flowers	175
The Babe	176
The Blanket	177
Puppy Love	178
The Little Horrors	179
The Lonely Field	180
Great Age	181
Habits	182
Traffic Lights	183
To Sleep or Not to Sleep	184
In the Whitehouse	185
Spendthrift	186
On the Internet	187

Always	188
Chubby Knees	189
November Mists	190
The House Next Door	191
Disaster Films	192
Cheer Leaders	193
The Black Cat	194
A Noisy Bird	195
Rock of Life	196
Loves Eternal Bond	197
Fireflies	198
Loneliness	199
Soft Mellow Light	200
Greedy Sun	201
Three Wise Men	202
The Watchers	203
Gifts	204
If I Could	205
Goodbye 2012	206
Loyalty	207
Happy Talk	208
The Witch	209
Whispering Winds	210
The Last Sunset	211
Dewdrops	212
Ten Books or More	213
The Stalker	214
Liquid Gold	215
The Fastest Gun	216
Tumbleweed	217
To Be a Mother	218
Waterworks	219
The Human Race	220
Shadow	221
Forever Run	222

Land of Umbrellas

This land of umbrellas
    Seems always wet and damp,
Held high above our heads
Is our user-friendly gamp.

The rain constantly drizzles
    Appearing every day,
Is this the English summer?
Which should be dry and gay.

Events are cancelled
    Due to muddy fields,
Will take more than umbrellas
To form an adequate shield.

The rain must cease sometime
    Cannot last for ever,
Indian summer is forecast
Not inclement weather.

So cheer up, it's not all bad
    Put on a grudging smile,
Lay down your umbrellas
At least for a little while.

It's Just Cricket

Upon the village playing field
    Teams strive to take a wicket,
Some batting, some bowling fast
    The age-old game of cricket.

A demon bowler hurls the ball
    That's bright shiny red,
The batsman tries to make some runs
    By thinking fast ahead.

The ball hits the bat full square
    It has missed the wicket,
A mighty swipe sends it soaring
    Right to the distant thicket.

In the cramped scoring hut
    Boys struggle to display,
Placing cards in special slots
    Longing for end of play.

The bowler rubs his trouser leg
    Supposed to speed the ball,
Relishing the tension caused
Until the stumps of wicket fall.

Jack of All Trades

It's said a little knowledge
    Can be a dangerous thing,
Decisions without wisdom
    Disasters soon can bring.

Our Jack of all trades
    Knew a little about a lot,
Bits of gathered lore
    Thrown into the pot.

Stirred up well in the mix
    Useful when required,
His assorted information
    Many a task inspired.

He appeared to be unfulfilled
    In spite of years of fun,
Scraps of data incomplete
    Left him master of none.

This wistful poignant saga
    Leaves me rather sad,
Jack tried to do his best
    But in mind, he was only a lad.

My Father

Hard working and mighty strong
    He was a handsome man,
With thick blond hair, bright blue eyes
    And healthy outdoor tan.

Worked hard hours and long
    Maintaining his rented farm,
Waites and Woodbines smoked outside
    Focused him and calmed.

Not allowed to smoke indoors
    It was the rule of Mum
Who never quite succeeded
    Keeping him under thumb.

I would have liked him to know
    How I truly admired him,
I could not get close enough to
    Indulge my childhood whim.

Alas it never happened
    The distance was maintained,
This gap in contact always meant
    I was the one he blamed.

Humidity

It is so flaming hot
Sun beats all day through,
There seems no reprieve
    For either me or you.

Perspiring, sticky,
All because of the humidity,
Bed covers on the body
    The height of stupidity.

Fast fans revolving
Aimed to cool the air,
The heat is so intense
    We hardly feel it there.

One thing will bring relief
Torrents of constant rain,
We long for the storm clouds
    To cool us down again.

Stifling humidity,
Too much for us to bare,
Overheating bodies,
    Nothing can compare!

Olympics

An international labour
    Entries all over the world,
Marching proudly to compete
    Flags and banners unfurled.

Archery and rowing events
    Held over many heats,
Famous faces taking part
    For medals they compete.

In the rowing regatta
    Really tough, hard work,
Needing lots of stamina
    No time to shirk.

The eventing with horses
    Over gruelling jumps,
The royal posterior
    Regally feels the bumps.

Zara rides her chestnut mount
    Looking good and strong,
A rider and horse show
    To delight the cheering throng.

White Fur

White fur on the carpet
White fur on the chair
He'd leave little presents
    To say he was there.

There can be no doubt
I'll miss my faithful friend,
I'm sure he always knew
    I loved him to the end.

I cannot believe, take it in
I've lost my beloved cat
One thing for certain
    He didn't deserve that.

I tried to say farewell
I mumbled my goodbyes,
I couldn't see properly
    The tears filled my eyes.

My Mischief not forgotten
Always in my mind,
I'll see the same pieces of
    White fur he left behind.

Bonfires

Not just part of November 5th
Bonfires burn all kinds of trash,
Making in the atmosphere a
    Murky, foggy hash.

Straight up to cleaner space
Sparks fly high,
Followed by roaring flames
    Send smoke to quickly lie.

Over the treetops lofty
Over the chimney pots,
Trailing above fields and
    Neat allotment plots.

There is no need for a guy
A-top the bonfire heap,
Just sparks and crackles heard
    As flames begin to leap.

Bonfires blaze fiercely away
And seem quite an oddity,
Yet getting rid of rubbish
    Proves a useful commodity.

Peas, Carrots and Taters

Favourites of the gardener
Who so carefully tends,
His earthly plot year round
    Whatever the weather sends.

Lovingly digging up the soil
To make it loose and light,
His plants will easier grow
    If leaves avoid the blight.

Some consumers of vegetables
Like peas, carrots and taters,
Young folk in particular
    Are Brussel-sprout haters.

But there is plenty of choice
Nothing is finer,
Fresh vegetables for lunch
    For the gourmet diner.

Munching away contentedly
Peas, carrots and taters,
Enjoyed by some daily
    Whenever the café caters.

Meat and two veg
The normal dinner platter,
Swamped by gravy rich
    Softens crisp roast taters.

The Red Planet

Red it glows in distant space
A planet amongst the stars,
Iron oxide in the soil shows
    The planet known as Mars.

Mars holds many secrets
One is called The Face,
The tomb of a warrior
    Staring up into space.

Once it had atmosphere
Many a waterway,
Encounter with object large
    Whipped the air away.

Probing from the earth
To Mars fourth from the sun,
Curiosity sent
    Pictures that surely stun.

One day we will explore
And on this planet tread,
Finding ancient signs of life
    Where creatures lived and bred.

The Dust Machine

In the field moves the combine
Reaping the ripened grain,
Kicking up clouds of dust
    To coat the car again.

Every year it is repeated
Great dust clouds are seen,
That's why its called
    The big dust machine.

When the sun is high
Then it seems far worse,
Bring on the evening cool
    To go into reverse.

When the field is finished
It's bare and lacking green,
'Til another year rolls round
    And we see the dust machine.

Oh for peace and quiet
Let us have our dreams,
Free from dust and noise
    Free from damned machines.

Writing, Writing, Writing

It was not an easy task
In a garret damp,
Trying to write volumes
    By dim light of lamp.

All good writers were poor
Never had a penny,
Short of food and clothing
    Yet their works were many.

The very best of drama
Was written by simple men,
Self-educated and keen
    Masters of the pen.

William Shakespeare, the bard
Did he really write his plays?
Some say his language was
    Too literate for those days.

Modern writers fantasise
Involving sorcery and magic,
Heroes performing feats
    Of rescues quite dramatic.

Lovers of mystery soak up
Crime stories galore,
Finding in the writings,
    An appetite for more.

The Village Church

Once more I see in my mind
The church where I was wed,
Solemnly I took my vows
Meant every word I said.

My father proudly took my arm,
Walking down the high aisle,
Family and friends looked on
Best suits, hats and smiles.

Right down the bottom
Is located an imposing tomb,
Dyer family since Norman times
Have laid there in the gloom.

Plaques to the fallen displayed
High in full view,
Many in World War One
One for World War Two.

There are two secret stairways
From the ground to up on high,
One leads to the belfry
The other out to the sky.

Many of the steps are missing
Broken over the years,
Climbers who take a chance
Stifle their worries and fears.

The Deep Blue Sea

Uncharted in many places
The deep blue sea,
Flows and ebbs precisely
    Veiled in mystery.

Greedy in demands for prey
Ships swiftly disappear,
Swallowed by the swelling waves
    Occurring every year.

A breeding ground for fish of
Such gigantic size,
Home of the monsters
    Down on the bottom lies.

Many an ancient sailor
Has found a watery grave,
Entreating, praying to gods
    Ship and lives to save.

Food for diverse masses
Meals of such clever creation,
Presenting simple to gourmet
    Such fare for our generation.

The Wasps

A wasp flew from the orchard
Leaving the colonies' nest,
Tucked high up in a tree
    A home for them to rest.

A young girl wandered by
And saw the nest up high,
Wasps she saw all abuzz
    And in the air did fly.

The owner of the orchard
Called the pest control,
Aiming to destroy the nest
    By gassing in the hole.

One lone hunter returned
To the nest now on the ground,
Dead wasps was all he saw
    That was all he found.

The girl skipped down the lane
She knew she should be glad,
But now the nest was gone
    Did feel a little sad.

Where Did I Put It?

Objects placed for keeping
In sideboard or down a chair,
Maybe in some secret drawer
    Of a cupboard up the stairs.

A bunch of keys laid down
Who can tell just where?
Were they thrown carelessly
    On a high or low shelf there.

Memory seems to falter
Even displays cruel flaws,
Years ago working, now
    Which of these many drawers?

Where did I put it?
Did I lock that door?
Why can't I remember
    Dropping it on the floor?

Is there some remedy
To aid forgetfulness?
Nothing has been found, to
    Stop such a cruel jest.

Butterflies

Silent graceful creatures
Like fairies gliding by,
Gossamer wings a-beating
    Hovers the butterfly.

Cousin of the night-time moth
Landing gently on the flowers,
To sip the nectar sweet
    For just a few short hours.

Peacocks, red admirals
Is to name but two,
Brimstones and fritillaries
    Kissed by the morning dew.

Flutterby is a better name
For these divine creatures,
Nothing to do with butter
    But magic work of nature.

On buddleias in the garden
A host of butterflies,
Complimenting the blooms
    Delightful to the eye.

Celestial Bridge

It is not a man-made structure
Spanning the skies to land,
Along which all can travel
    From the humble to the grand.

When our earthly body quits
Ceasing its long-term fight,
The spirit goes to the bridge
    Enveloped in new light.

It would seem the crossing point
Is way up in the skies,
Journey to celestial space
    For the spirit never dies.

Wanting, seeking explanation
Questions will arise,
Have we been bamboozled?
    And told a load of lies.

Celestial bridge is real enough
Touching down on land,
After storms it's always there
    A bridge of shining bands.

The Boss

It's a complex, grim position
To head a thriving firm,
Takes years of experience and
    Many hard lessons to learn.

The good boss always listens
With ever open door,
Willing to solve works' queries
    And of staff, the more.

Often we have a female
Taking on the boss's part,
Her role will demonstrate
    Head must rule the heart.

Generating income is
In the hands of the boss,
The workers' cooperation
    Ensures it runs without loss.

The boss on duty all the time
At customer's beck and call,
Has to delegate some tasks
    Or he's no boss at all.

Nuts

The acorn fruit of the oak trees
Majestically ripening nuts
Clustered high on leafy boughs
    Snug in their birth-wrought cups.

Hearts of oak we sung their praise
Proud of our tenacity,
We never give in to bullies
    For England must be free.

Planting acorns that will grow
Strongly to mighty oaks,
They will symbolise
    That England always copes.

Strong and hardy woods
From little acorns grow,
Thriving in English soil,
    Their oak-born strength they show.

The nuts in a cup best describes
The unique fruits of the oak,
Nuts, also might apply to leaders
    In the house that rules our folk.

Cattle Drive

Every autumn we moved the cows
To the water-meadows lea,
Bordering the river, they
    Munched contentedly.

Heavy autumn rains
Caused the river to swell
Bursting its banks
    Flooding the fields as well.

The cows were marooned
On small strip of high land,
They must be moved ere
    Things got out of hand.

A big lorry was driven
To the flooded river site,
It was hard to park up
    In the fading autumn light.

Could we load the cows in time?
Drive them through the water,
Into the cattle truck
    Before the vehicle faltered.

Finally the effort paid off
The cows were loaded on,
Now we had to smartly move
    Pack up and be gone.

We had saved the day
The cows were all alive,
Bumping backwards and forwards
    In an autumn cattle drive.

On The Carpet

Being on the carpet
Means you are in trouble,
Have to grin and bear it
    And wish you had a double.

Furniture on the carpet
Needs to be placed on pads,
Avoiding indentations
    From hefty lass and lads.

Pets can mar the carpet
Leaving their ugly stain,
Rubbing in the culprit's nose
    Stops repeat of same.

Some say carpets can fly
High over land and seas,
A tale of eastern magic
    Listeners' ears to please.

Love made on the carpet
A worthy art to learn,
Too vigorous an action
    Can cause a friction burn.

The Message of Flowers

In flowers words need not express
    What the intention should be,
The beauty of fragrant blooms
    Cut from bed, shrub or tree.

Dark red roses, a sign of love
    Used to show much more,
Given by knight to his lady
    Way back in days of yore.

To smell the scent of flowers
    Transports one to bliss,
Coupled with the hope
    Soon will come a kiss.

When rain falls from the skies
    Heavy hang the flowers,
Dripping down to the roots
    Fed by frequent showers.

The message of flowers
    Is abundantly clear,
'Tis love declared simply
    In ways we cannot hear.

The Babe

On a blue water planet
In September morning clear,
Was born a wailing baby
    On a hill in Bedfordshire.

The infant girl was healthy
Unlike her sister gone,
A problem to her parents
    Because she was not a son.

Her cottage home was bleak
More like a draughty barn,
Her father worked round the clock
    To keep the little farm.

She grew up running wild
In the fields of wheat and oats,
Her friends were the animals
    Cuddling their hairy coats.

Born a year before the war
Rationing came into force,
Meat was so very scarce
    Beef more like stringy horse.

She soaked up learning
Questioned the laid down word,
The child knew her queries
    Were ignored and never heard.

She became a business woman,
Her efforts were applauded,
For seeking still the answers
    Her questions were rewarded.

The Blanket

Tumbling down from the heavens
    Gently, softly without sound,
Snowflakes fall in flurries
    A blanket covering the ground.

Smooth, levelling the view
    There are no ups or downs,
All is crisp and even
    Covering countryside and town.

Settling through the night
    Not a mark is seen,
Come morning there are slots
    Where rabbit and deer have been.

Hiding from the winter cold
    No where else to go,
Little creatures crouch unseen
    In the land of winter snow.

Food is scarce, demand is great
    Foraging works abound,
Until the springtime thaw
    Melts the blanket on the ground.

Puppy Love

The love of man for his friend
Or love of youth for a girl,
The first flush of emotions
    Leaving your head in a whirl.

There is nothing that can compare
To the sturdy strong bond,
Formed 'twix man and his dog
    Be it black, tan, or blonde.

Loyalty of the highest order
Exists between the two,
When one departs this life
    What does the other do?

The answer is so simple,
Get back on the horse and ride,
Find another canine love
    To take the place of pride.

Honour your former friend
With enduring firm affection,
That only you can give
    Puppy love's perfection.

The Little Horrors

We have two small puppies
Messy little horrors,
We just hope that it will
    Be better by tomorrow.

We have a dog and sister
A pretty little bitch,
At present 'tis very hard
    To tell which is which.

The bitch is the larger and
More bossy of the two,
An eating factory
    That always end in poo!

Messes here and messes there
Careful where we tread,
We long for them to be
    House-trained instead.

Into all and everything
Nothing is safe in their reach,
Patience is sorely needed
    Their training so to teach.

Their little teeth are so sharp
Needles piecing our skin,
Why don't they just use their chews?
    Gnawing from thick to thin.

We want the weeks to pass
So, when they've grown up
We should have handsome dogs
    Not little horror pups.

The Lonely Field

Wheat harvested and carted away
    The straw baled in squares,
Stubble ploughed in the ground
Now the field is bare.

No crops flourish in its soil
    No harvest mice play on stalks,
No small birds catching grain
Only rooks parade and squawk.

The field waits now for spring
    When plants will grow again,
First it must endure the winter
Frost, snows, and icy rain.

'Til the tractor's engine sounds
    Towing the seed corn drill,
Up and down the lonely field
Planting new grain at will.

Bare and bleak the field lays
    Its living heart asleep,
Until the coming hour
When, once more it will beat.

Great Age

Some people seem to relish
And boast of a great age,
Wallowing in the years past
    Others turn a fresh page.

Some suffer many aches and pains
And cannot find the cause,
Remedies have little effect
    Giving just a pause.

It is a great pity
For a young, able man,
To go down hill rapidly
    His fitness down the pan.

The only way is forward
Put faith in inner strength,
Just pour a stiff drink
    And use your common sense.

Over the passing years
Much knowledge is a gain,
But life is burdensome
    Our bodies hosts to pain.

Great age means living long
Learning all the time,
Until accumulated lore
    Eases the uphill climb.

Habits

Some of us on the first of the month
Will say "white rabbits",
We do not really know why
    It's just a childhood habit.

On the other hand monks and friars
Wear garments known as habits,
Simple garb covering all
    Nothing to do with rabbits.

Habits are subconscious things
We remember as a child,
Some quaint, some are nasty
    Should in the bin be piled.

Scratching one's rear end
An example of the bad,
Do we merely need a wash?
    Or simply going mad?

Some folk affect their voice
Hoping to elevate,
Their position in society
    In fact it irritates.

Why do we say white rabbits?
We cannot fathom why,
A habit handed down
    And we simply comply.

Traffic Lights

Wait here when red light shows
So says the traffic control,
A token placed in position
    Just guarding an empty hole.

For days on end it seems
The lights stay firmly there,
No work is going on
    No surface being repaired.

Why put them out so soon
Before the work is ready?
Motorists become irate
    Their foot on brake unsteady.

When lights are used to control
Traffic jams in busy towns,
Well chosen means to direct
    Mr and Mrs Brown.

The ordinary motorist
Obeys green, amber and red,
Wishing to avoid
    The risk of hospital bed.

So just wait patiently
Sit watching in the queue,
Hoping the lights will soon change
    And your vehicle can go through.

To Sleep or Not to Sleep

After a hard day's labour
Our body craves for sleep,
Charging our low energy
    With slumber soft and deep.

If our sleep is broken
Ratty we become,
To cure the nagging reason
    Should be the rule of thumb.

The most common cause of
A disturbed night's rest,
Is noise that irks our senses
    Some scurrying little pest.

Or is it that our bed's at fault?
We cannot position right,
We toss and turn many times
    It seems throughout the night.

Bed too hard, bed too soft
Backache reigns supreme,
Buy another mattress
    To get a pleasant dream.

Always money to try for change
Is there no outlay's end?
Only an open purse it seems
    Again to spend, spend, spend!

In the Whitehouse

Elections are now over
There is no new resident,
Back to the same old recipe
There is no change in President.

The oval office rules America
Guided by the Democrats,
But they need cooperation
From Republican bureaucrats.

Will Americans unite in force
And henceforth pull together?
Hurricane Sandy proved a strain
With its terrible weather.

America leads the world
In humanitarian aid,
But can rush in too soon
So, many mistakes are made.

Friendly fire, there's no such thing
How can such fire be friendly?
Maiming one's own personnel
Mistaken for the enemy.

So, the occupant of the Whitehouse
Must be a man of skill,
A true friend of Great Britain
Cherishing our firm goodwill.

Spendthrift

It does not pay to save
To be taxed on it twice,
Money hard earned, taxed at source
    Taxes squeezing like a vice.

Save a bit and be taxed again
Why not spend the lot?
There is no reason not to
    As no one cares a jot.

The spendthrift enjoys his life
Buying up all he sees,
Hoarding, stuffing cupboards
    With goods designed to tease.

At the end of his life comes trouble
Piled up bills and debts,
He hardly blinks an eyelid
    Nor breaks out in a sweat.

Mr Spendthrift quits this life
Still owing the revenue,
Death duties levied on his estate
    Leaving his family blue.

But he had a good life
Knew how to have fun,
As Bob Cratchits small child said
    "God bless us everyone."

On the Internet

Repeat this and repeat that
What is the secret code?
Do it once more to see
    If the programme will load.

No, it does not on first attempt
You try to work it out,
Fed up, you find yourself
    Having to rage and shout.

So, you try again
Now, will it display?
Then suddenly, despair
    Screen has blanked away.

Being a persistent soul
You refuse to give up,
Enter it all once more
    Accurate, short and abrupt.

Eureka! the screen's lit up
The data is visible there,
You can stop fretting
    And tearing out your hair.

Pleased with a result at last
Proudly you peer, then scream,
For useless data by the ton
    Is cluttering up your screen.

Always

My love for you is eternal
Today, tomorrow, always,
Formed by our meeting years ago
    For the remainder of my days.

In spite of some differences
I balance them up and down,
Realising what a fool I am
    My face in tears I drown.

Being a sensitive soul
Quite a burden it can be,
To understand both sides
    And trying too hard to see –

Why an action has been taken
Why some words were spoken,
I'll always put you first
    I pray and keep on hoping.

Maybe, in time I will spend
My final night in bed,
With you there beside me
    Your arms cradling my head.

Today, tomorrow, always
My love constant and true,
To the end of my life on earth
    No one else but you.

Chubby Knees

He sits in his chair
Rubbing his chubby knees,
Trousers around his ankles
    A sight contrived to please!

So, the sight may be amusing
Legs cold enough to freeze?
Now he's had an accident
    And banged his chubby knees.

The essence of embrocation
Wafts strongly on the breeze,
That's created by the draughts
    Causing my nose to sneeze.

His firm legs like English oak
Pain shoots up his calf once more,
Hope the medication penetrates
    Rapidly through skin and pore.

After rubbing good and hard
Into his painful knees,
Remains of the stuff drying out
    Smells like ripe old cheese.

November Mists

November mist blankets the land
And soon must roll away,
Yielding to the icy cold
    Of the bleak December days.

The mist muffles all the sound
In a cloak of murky grey,
Slowing traffic to a snail's pace
    Creeping down the motorway.

Warning lights to cut speed
A prudent exercise,
Going fast through the fog
    Sensibility defies.

Water drips from the trees
Soaking cattle, sheep and goats,
Penetrating to their skin
    Through their hairy coats.

So November fades away
And December arrives to close
The year, with its bitter cold
    Seasonal Christmas snows.

The House Next Door

The house next door is empty
Our friendly neighbours gone,
The house is for sale
    We hope not empty for long.

The house is a cottage
With authentic wooden beams,
A cosy homely interior
    Fittings and fixtures gleam.

The drive has little room
For the parking of cars,
The garage door's too tight
    To squeeze between the bars.

A couple of fraudsters moving in
Were rumbled by the agents,
The owner got there just in time
    So again, the cottage is vacant.

So back to square one
The house is on the market,
We need a decent family
    Not some cheating basket.

Disaster Films

There seems to be rather a lot
Of disaster movies on TV,
I'm such a quivering coward
    These I do not wish to see.

People trapped far underground
All hoping for rescue,
Some will scramble to the top
    Squashing others in the queue.

Or fire raging in a shop
Sweeping from floor to floor,
Firemen's rescue ladders
    Reach to the flaming store.

A volcano erupts suddenly
Gas and molten rock sweep down,
Residents must fast evacuate
    Before it engulfs their town.

An aeroplane is in trouble
Threatened by a bomb on board,
Planted by terrorists, who
    Used to use the sword.

So, I avoid watching films
That depict such gloom,
For we do not relish
    Thinking this could be our doom.

Stuff and nonsense some will say
This is not reality,
Fate is written in the stars
    And for some, it will be.

Cheer Leaders

Two, four, six, eight
Whom do we appreciate?
An age-old sing-song rhyme
    Chanting on the touch line.

Egging on their team to win
Jumping up and down,
Screaming on the boundary
    These girls so noisy sound.

Fans of opposing teams
Almost hysterical,
Mock and jeer each other
    Their antics crudely physical.

Teen girls nearly faint
At sight of heroes brawny,
But sometimes the winners
    Are brainy chaps quite scrawny.

All through the actual game
Cheerleaders are performing,
Other spectators, so fed up
    Want their display to reform.

Most folk are sick to death
Of these teenage high kickers,
Who work up to a frenzy
    Until they wet their knickers.

The Black Cat

A black cat visits our garden
Sometimes twice or more a day,
I wonder where she lives
    Or is she just a stray?

I love pussy cats most dearly
But alas, now I have none,
I long to fuss another
    As my lovely cats are gone.

This little cat in the garden
So cuddly and so neat,
I often see her munching
    Bits, we throw her to eat.

She must belong to somebody
Surely they must miss her?
Why don't they mount a search?
    To find and hear her purr.

I would strongly like to keep her
But have to entice her near,
Yet fleet of foot she runs away
    Scared and full of fear.

Now has she been mistreated?
If I knew I'd be so sad,
For such cruelty illustrates
    Some people are nasty and bad.

A Noisy Bird

At first light in the countryside
An alarm call loud is heard,
It comes from the farmyard's
    Noisy rooster bird.

He stretches out his neck
And crows to wake us all,
It's time to arise
    When we hear his call.

In Bible times of long ago
Peter was told by Christ,
"You will betray me Peter
    Ere the cock crows thrice."

And so it came to pass
In the garden of Gethsemane,
Peter denied Jesus and so
    Betrayed him to the enemy.

The farmyard cockerel proud
Rounds up his hens and crows,
Telling all, these are mine
    Warding off potential foes.

Puffing out his chest
Again and again he calls,
Many weary workers
    Don't like the sound at all.

Rock of Life

A man wand'ring in the desert
Struck a rock with his staff,
The rock gushed forth water
    Pouring down the stony path.

The precious elixir of life
Needed by all humankind,
Only a little in the desert
    For travellers to find.

The man was tired and weary
Almost dying of thirst,
How did a single blow
    Make the rock face burst?

Just where the staff hit the rock
There was a fragile fracture,
Holding back the water
    Against the laws of nature.

No treasure map to guide him
A star caught his watching eye,
And caused this lone parched
    Trekker to halt, not walk by.

Modern-day explorers
Have failed to find the place,
Where life-giving water
    Pours from the bare rock face.

Loves Eternal Bond

It is not conjured by a wizard
From a waving of his wand,
It is forged by understanding
    Is love's eternal bond.

It will go on through the ages
Firm and strong for ever,
Anyone can own it
    No need to be clever.

It takes two to tango
It takes two to fall in love,
To form a lasting union
    To fit like hand in glove.

Tolerate the shortcomings
That applies to us all,
See more than one angle
    'Cos pride goes before a fall.

Your lady may just be right
Feel your strong love's bond,
It will endure any problems
    Be she brunette or blonde.

Time to display emotion
Open up and respond,
Embrace the person who shares
    Love's eternal bond.

Fireflies

In the late evening light
Insect clouds fall and rise,
A glowing type of beetle
    We know to be fireflies.

Why do they shine at night
These beetles without sound,
Only the tail part glows
    The rest a dirty brown.

The male needs to find a mate
So puts on his display,
Can only be seen in the dark
    Not by light of day.

It always works
A female bug arrives,
He catches her and mates
    To live out simple lives.

The evening skies are lit
By the fireflies' dance,
A rare sight to appreciate
    One designed to enchant.

Many species do not trouble
To attract a lady fair,
The firefly male shines forth
    His female mate to ensnare.

Loneliness

Who can know the anguish
That isolation brings?
No one is there, no one to share
    The telephone never rings.

Sole contact with the outside world
Only a bill on the mat,
Delivered by the postman
    Quickly pushed through the flap.

The house is too big and empty
No one there, sharing the home,
Dust covers many rooms
    Just one person living alone.

Television helps pass the time
Showing family circles and friends,
Similar to old memories
    But there the likeness ends.

I was lonely many years ago
Husband gone, Mother died.
Went out for the sake of it
    Buckets of tears I cried.

We all end being lonely
And afraid of future times,
Remember, life can change
    With subtlety sublime.

Soft Mellow Light

There are various kinds of glare
The harshness of peak summer bright,
The contrasting blindness
    Achieved by winter's white.

When it is dark we are lost
Fumbling our way in fright,
Illumination is needed
    By way of mellow light.

Neither too hot or cold
We yearn for the sight,
Of the sun shining softly
    Putting the world to rights.

Such gentleness comes in autumn
Days are warm and short,
All of this is governed
    By the sun's lunar consort.

Light from the moon is silver
Sufficient through the night,
To illuminate our journey
    With its soft mellow light.

Greedy Sun

Though our world may turn to ashes,
Devoured by a greedy sun,
The star that has nurtured us
    Since before time begun.

Long has the sun favoured us
With benevolent rays,
But it will withdraw its blessing
    When comes the end of days.

Depleted in its energy
Will seek to find a supply,
Earth will be a target for
    The sun on which we rely.

Summertime and winter
Daytime and darkest night,
Seedtime and garnering
    All children of the light.

When the sun has gone
Can mankind survive?
By finding another planet
    That will support human life.

Out there in the universe
Perhaps are suitable spheres,
Able to take our species
    On open fertile frontiers.

Three Wise Men

The Magi, as they were known
Learned men of their time,
Found they needed help
    To find the Child Divine.

'Tis said they came from the east
And followed a guiding star,
If they were so very wise
    They should have known the path –

That lead them to the place,
And gone there directly,
A humble stable cave
    Was home for this family.

On arrival they saw the infant Christ,
Presented their precious gifts,
Then had to avoid the hand
    Of King Herod's swift fist.

They escaped from his trap
Leaving the infant there,
The star once more their guide
    A shining symbol in the air.

The Watchers

As the shepherds kept watch
Over their gathered flock,
The hill suddenly lit up
    Exposing sheep, men and rock.

Scared then, were these men
And some felt quite ill,
Frozen to the spot they stood
    Without strength or will.

When they dared look upwards
Saw an object in the air,
Hovering far above them
    And the light came from there.

In their minds they heard a voice
Telling them to be firm,
Feel the force all around them
    No need to cringe or squirm.

Thus, they were told a story
They'd a task to undertake,
For those simple shepherds
    A journey must make.

So they made their way and found
Bethlehem's little town,
And saw the new-born king
    His head, without a crown.

Gifts

Problems with buying gifts
Unsure what to get?
For those choosy teenagers
    Who now surf the net.

Advertisements abound
On radio and TV,
Shops and magazines
    So much to hear and see.

Unless one drops a hint
On what they would really like,
One flounders in the dark
    Without the faintest light.

It really is a problem
Not wishing to offend,
So you hope for the best
    With the gifts you send.

Or if you feel downhearted
When you've tried so hard,
Pour yourself a drink
    And just send them a card.

If I Could

If I could a wish be granted
And reverse the march of time,
I would like to be nineteen
    When my life was fine.

I had many occupations
Really loved my posts,
By learning from professionals
    I was better paid than most.

In haste I married a man
Of qualities unknown,
Mistakenly, I assumed
    His love was like my own.

If I could untie that knot
Gladly I'd take that step,
Taking much more time
    Wishing I could forget.

Rushing into situations
Just to have a lark,
I could have chosen better
    Ways to make my mark.

My parents and rigid ways
Kept me where they would,
I ached to improve myself
    As I knew I could.

If I could undo the past
I would cut out speed,
Gently taking life
    As slowly as I need.

Goodbye 2012

As the old year rolls to a close
So we must say goodbye,
Musing on the last twelve months
    With deep nostalgic sighs.

Believed ending of the world
In December's third week,
The Mayan calendar stops
    Mankind's survival was bleak.

Yet it was not so ordained
Earthly life continued,
The world turned as before,
    And we all could breathe anew.

So we can reflect in peace,
Look forward to thirteen,
Enjoy our leisure hours
    With gallons of hot caffeine.

Cups of steaming tea
And percolated coffee,
Will make us realise
    And appreciate liberty.

We all just need to see
The blessings we receive
Should continue in the future
    As this old year we leave.

Loyalty

I do not wish to write
A poem about Valentine,
Too much the same's been said
    So I'm not inclined.

Drivel of love and roses red
Swearing adoration true,
Let's be down to earth
    I'm bonded fast to you.

Last year was a disaster
Emotionally and health,
Death of our pets came,
    Like a thunderbolt of stealth.

There is no magic formulae
That can put things right,
Tender hearts still ache
    Longing for another sight –

Of furry friends, cat and dog
Companions, loyal and true,
Never wavering in their love
    So protective, so faithful.

Happy Talk

Not merely a spoken language
Rather, it sounds as sung,
With pleasant ups and downs
    The true Welsh mother tongue.

Banned by an English King
The directive was not obeyed,
Cherished and well protected
    This happy talk stayed –

Deep in the hearts of the Welsh
Keeping its spirit alive,
Bards and male voice choirs
    Ensured it would survive.

To the foreign ear
The language is unique,
Warmly entertaining
    Just to hear them speak.

There is nothing to match it
These special happy words,
From the Welsh valleys
    A voice that must be heard.

The Witch

She lived in a crooked cottage
    In the woods' deepest part,
Using age-old talents
    She dabbled in black arts.

She had a jet black cat
    Last of a long line similar,
It followed her around the house
    And slept as her familiar.

She mixed herbs and powders
    To make hoards of pills,
To local folk she possessed
    A cure for all their ills.

Many a maid in trouble
    Came to seek abortion,
She did her best for the girl
    Treating her with caution.

A travelling witch-finder
    Heard of this old crone,
He found her guilty
    Sacked and burned her home.

But she was not in the cottage
    So escaped the flames,
Local folk rebuilt her cot'
    And she carried on the same.

For they had realised
    They would miss her potent spells,
All through her many years
    She'd treated them, and well.

Whispering Wind

One by one the petals of a flower
Slowly drop to the ground,
Softly, gently gliding
    Landing without a sound.

So comes the whispering wind
Friendly, warm and benign,
Telling tales of people
    And places left far behind.

Quietly the wind rustles,
Vibrating the chestnut trees,
Sending conker bombs plunging,
    Waiting children to please.

The whispering wind is welcomed
By the soft green shoots,
Unlike the winter's gales
    That bluster and uproot –

The weakest growing shrubs,
And the heathers that cling.
The warm whispering wind
    Heralds the coming spring.

The Last Sunset

When this earth is tired of spinning
And mankind is under threat,
We must find another habitat
    Before the last sunset.

Our hitherto friendly sun
Will prove to be hostile,
Scorching planets one by one
    Turning their surface vile.

Earth will be on the list
In line to be absorbed,
Burned to a dead cinder
    That cannot be restored.

As the sun comes nearer
Humans begin to sweat,
Their quaking limbs demonstrate
    They just can't forget.

They gambled in the belief
Preached from every pulpit,
The world would spin for ever
    As long as man was fit –

To take his place with the gods
High on Mount Olympus,
A world of myth and worship
    Taught the primitive and curious.

Dewdrops

A dewdrop rolled
Stopped and hung,
Sparkling, to see
    Lit by the sun.

Remaining suspended
A hanging tear,
Caught one moment
    To then disappear.

Winter dewdrops
Falling below,
Off laurel leaves
    Puncturing the snow.

Dewdrops we see
A moment in time,
Gems in sunlight
    Sparklers sublime.

Rare is the glimpse
Of dewdrops bringing,
Nature's bright joy
    Of dewdrops clinging.

Ten Books or More?

When we started writing
Our books of rhyming lines,
We went into production
    Now we're up to nine.

One book was not enough
We had so much to say,
Putting thoughts on paper
    Mainly every day.

Separately we create
Loving every moment,
Baring innermost souls
    By variety of content.

We feel most strongly
For animal welfare,
Getting really riled
    At owners' lack of care.

They really do not deserve
To be in charge of creatures,
We would hand out the same
    Bad treatment they meter.

We love an' care for animals,
And say so in our books,
Places in our jails
    Should await these no goods.

So we go on writing
Sometimes quite profound,
Our books exalt nature
    Wherever it is found.

The Stalker

Product of a twisted mind
Corruption in a brain,
The stalker wishes nothing but
    Torture and great pain.

His aim has festered long
Now it's an obsession,
His victim has become
    A coveted possession.

He watches and he waits
'Til victim is at home,
Then he constantly rings
    The resident telephone.

The victim answers many times
As it rings in the night,
Silence at the other end brings
    On a panic attack of fright.

Rustling in shadows outside
Unnerving, to the viewer,
Ways to stop the plague
    Options getting fewer –

Police or counsel say
Try to be accompanied,
That will stop the prowler's
    Interference bid.

Protesting if caught
Giving excuses so lame,
He has a medical condition
    And is really not to blame.

Liquid Gold

The sun shines in winter time
In beams of liquid gold,
Yet without true strength
    To overcome the cold.

The rays are weak in heat
The winter winds are strong,
Coming from the frozen North
    The home where they belong.

Still the sun shines on
Into winter's morn,
Bringing a little warmth
    To lambs newly born.

Dropped in the winter night
In a humble fellside fold,
Their survival depends
    On bands of liquid gold –

Melting the icy bank to run
Trickling into the stream,
Nature's water of life
    Pure, in sunlight's gleam.

Pure gold upon the grey
And biting wind relates
To cold, yet round the corner
    More liquid gold awaits.

The Fastest Gun

In America's cowboy era
Shooting rivalry and tests,
Took place just to see
    Which man was the fastest.

Who could outshoot the other
All part of the Wild West,
Legendary accuracy shows
    The toughest men were best.

They tried to maintain
Some law and order,
Chasing fleeing outlaws
    To the Mexican border.

Many baddies were not alone
They also rode in gangs,
Raided far and wide
    And many then were hanged.

The fastest gun's reputation
Followed where'er he roamed,
Found he could not possess
    A family or home.

Always someone to challenge
Boasted to their peers,
They could end the fame
    Held for so many years.

The fastest gun had no choice
But to wander on,
One town to another
    Until his days were done.

Tumbleweed

Blowing across the desert
Are clumps of tumbleweed,
Its shallow roots makes sure
    It never goes to seed.

Tumbling up or down the streets
Of many a Western town,
This plant symbolises
    Freedom where it's blown.

Nothing to tie it down
No root to keep its place,
Blowing up the railroads
    Whirling into space.

To fall as the wind eases
Floating to the ground,
Stopping in the stations
    For moments where it's found.

The envy of prisoners
Who long to be freed,
Why can't they drift away
    Just like the tumbleweed.

But they cannot tumble so
They have to pay for crimes,
And when the desert wind blows
    They must all stay behind.

To Be a Mother

There is no stronger bond
Than to be a mother,
Undefinable in quality
    Replaced by no other.

For some mothers
The act of giving birth,
Brings pain in labour
    Questioning its worth?

Was it really a good thing?
Bringing forth a new child
With years of servitude and
    Soiled nappies by the pile.

Nature has a knack
Of making it seem OK,
Feeding every few hours
    All night and all day.

Comes the time at last
Of an unbroken night,
Followed by the first smile
    A little face all alight.

To be a mother
Brings tiredness and stress,
But all fades away
    For we realise we're blessed.

Waterworks

Able to turn them on at will
Some persons use as a weapon,
Screwing up their lovely face
    Someone just to threaten.

If you don't give in at once
Comes a long campaign of tears,
Aimed to wear you down
    By playing on your fears.

Waterworks are a service
Providing our drinking fluid
Purifying through many filters
    A murky and cloudy liquid.

Expensive process in all
Depending on river levels,
Rainfall into the streams
    In which the fishes revel.

This end product, our drink
Has cost the household dear,
They hope that the drinking water
    Will remain pure and clear.

They are so unlike
False tears versus clear stream,
One is quenching water
    The other a stupid scheme.

The Human Race

What is this mad scramble
We call the human race?
Housing too close to each other
    As we try to save space.

We also go upwards
High-rise flats to see,
Little boxes to live in
    Hell for the family.

Poor sound insulation
Cold and poorly heated,
Residents down and dejected
    All their dreams deleted.

So we created a nightmare
Humans in near squalor,
Only other planets bring
    Chance of a fresh tomorrow.

We must not make the same mistakes
As on this planet here,
Crowding our living quarters
    With buildings much too near.

Getting away from earth
Could see us polluting space,
A very sad indictment
    Of all the human race.

Shadow

I have a cat to love once more
Shadow is his name,
He is black and furry
    Friendly and very tame.

His long and glossy coat
Sports just a few white hairs,
His eyes like bright diamonds
    As straight at me he stares.

He prefers dried food
And variety of cat treats,
Nibbled a few at a time
    He's fussy what he eats.

His former owner must have spoiled
And pampered him quite rotten,
I hope he will soon adapt
    And bad habits soon forgotten.

He likes to hide away
Underneath a cupboard shelf,
With a lot of coaxing
    He will come to myself.

After a few minutes
Back he hides again,
Right into the corner
    Choosing to remain.

Forever Run

Each single beat in the hall
The timepiece's tick-tock,
Should make us all think
    Realise and take stock.

Each single second
Is gone for ever,
Cannot be brought back
    Not even by the clever.

Each minute is precious
And so should be cherished,
By every person alive
    Ere we all wane and perish.

Life is for living
Each second slips away,
Going we know not where
    Forever to decay.

It is the same with writers
When the writing's done,
The pen is laid down
    It's written work now run.